A Gentleman Gets Dressed Up

Other GentleManners Books

How to Be a Gentleman
John Bridges

A Gentleman Entertains
John Bridges and Bryan Curtis

As a Gentleman Would Say
John Bridges and Bryan Curtis

How to Be a Lady
Candace Simpson-Giles

How to Raise a Lady
Kay West

How to Raise a Gentleman
Kay West

A Gentleman Raises His Glass
John Bridges and Bryan Curtis

A Gentleman Pens a Note
John Bridges and Bryan Curtis

A Gentleman Gets Dressed Up

WHAT TO WEAR
WHEN TO WEAR IT
HOW TO WEAR IT

JOHN BRIDGES
AND
BRYAN CURTIS

Viva Books

New Delhi | Mumbai | Chennai | Kolkata | Bangalore | Hyderabad | Kochi

First Indian Edition 2004
Reprinted 2008

VIVA BOOKS PRIVATE LIMITED

- 4737/23 Ansari Road, Daryaganj, New Delhi 110 002
  E-mail: vivadelhi@vivagroupindia.net, Tel. 42242200
- Plot No. 76, Service Industries, Shirvane, Sector 1, Nerul, Navi Mumbai 400 706,
  E-mail: vivamumbai@vivagroupindia.net, Tel. 27721273, 27721274
- Jamals Fazal Chambers, 26 Greams Road, Chennai 600 006
  E-mail: vivachennai@vivagroupindia.net, Tel. 28290304, 28294241
- B-103, Jindal Towers, 21/1A/3 Darga Road, Kolkata 700 017
  E-mail: vivakolkata@vivagroupindia.net, Tel. 22836381, 22816713
- 7, Sovereign Park Apartments, 56-58, K. R. Road, Basavanagudi, Bangalore 560 004
  E-mail: vivabangalore@vivagroupindia.net, Tel. 26607409, 26607410
- 101-102 Mughal Marc Apartments, 3-4-637 to 641, Narayanguda, Hyderabad 500 029
  E-mail: vivahyderabad@vivagroupindia.net, Tel. 27564481, 27564482
- First Floor, Beevi Towers, SRM Road, Kaloor, Kochi 682 018, Kerala
  E-mail: vivakochi@vivagroupindia.net, Tel: 0484-2403055, 2403056

Published by arrangement with

Rutledge Hill Press
A division of Thomas Nelson, Inc.
PO Box 141000, Nashville
Tennessee 37214

ISBN-10: 81-7649-924-2
ISBN-13: 978-81-7649-924-8

Published by Vinod Vasishtha for Viva Books Private Limited, 4737/23, Ansari Road, New Delhi 110 002. Printed and bound by Raj Press, R-3, Inderpuri, New Delhi - 110 012.

For Sally Levine,
who has little, if any,
time for stuffed shirts
—J.B.

For Mindy Henderson
and Staci Joyce,
for years of compliments
and friendship
—B.C.

CONTENTS

Introduction ix

A GENTLEMAN FROM HEAD TO TOE 13

Hats and Caps 15

Haircuts and Grooming 24

Ties and Other Neckware 34

Shirts, Collars, and Cuffs 53

Trousers 63

Suits, Blazers, and Sports Coats 70

Formalwear 80

Shoes 98

The Finishing Touches 109

A GENTLEMAN FOR ALL OCCASIONS 129

A Gentleman Gets Dressed for a Wedding 132

A Gentleman Gets Dressed for a Cocktail Party 138

A Gentleman Gets Dressed for a Funeral 140

A Gentleman Gets Dressed for a Religious Service 141

A Gentleman Gets Dressed for a Job Interview 142

A Gentleman Gets Dressed for a Concert 143

A Gentleman Gets Dressed for a Cookout 144

A Gentleman Gets Dressed for a Night on the Town 145

A Gentleman Gets Dressed for a White-Tie Fundraiser 146

A Gentleman Gets Dressed for a Masked Ball 148

A Gentleman Gets Ready for a Party 149

A GENTLMAN TAKES CARE OF HIS CLOTHES 151

A GENTLEMAN GOES SHOPPING 157

A GENTLEMAN IS ONLY HUMAN 171

INTRODUCTION

If a gentleman is wise, he is grateful that there are rules about a few things in life. He is particularly grateful that some of those rules apply to what he may wear or may not wear when he is lucky enough to be included in life's special occasions. Even the most seasoned gentleman may find himself thinking twice before he begins to dress. Being a gentleman, he does not want to stand out in the crowd—even if the crowd is a festive one, like the revelers at a black-tie ball, and especially if the gathering is a somber one, such as the funeral of a coworker. The gentleman desires simply to dress appropriately for the occasion—be it high-spirited and convivial or dignified and ceremonial.

A gentleman takes care that he looks his best, and dresses his best, every day, since he never knows when he will meet his next major client or the love of his life. He understands that good grooming—like any other aspect of the gentlemanly life—is not a matter of money.

He does not have to run up the balances on his credit cards just to keep his shoes neatly shined, his sports coat brushed, and his hair neatly trimmed. Even if his wardrobe is limited, he knows that as long as it is carefully selected and well cared for, it can take him—and he can take it—to life's most challenging occasions. He can be confident that as long as his closet contains a few staples, he is ready to dress and head out the door at a moment's notice.

But even if he gives little thought to his appearance from day to day, and even if he has no intention of accepting an invitation to anybody's black-tie party, every gentleman knows that the moment will come when he must pay attention to which shirt he puts on his back, which jacket he dons on top of it, and perhaps even which tie he knots around his neck. This book provides detailed guidance to help the gentleman face each of life's sartorial challenges—whether it is his college roommate's wedding, a cookout with friends from the office, or his own high-pressured interview for a new job.

With these guidelines, even a gentleman who

has been branded an inveterate "slob" can transform himself, at least on select occasions, into the tasteful, well-mannered fellow Nature intended him to be. At such moments, in fact, he may surprise himself as to how good it feels to look his best. He may even decide to make it a habit, transforming each of life's occasions somehow into a special one.

That, after all, is part of his ultimate job as a gentleman. When it comes to getting dressed, it is not a gentleman's goal to stand out from the crowd. He is confident that his intelligence, his resourcefulness, his hearty handshake, and his ready smile set him apart from all others. His clothes, he knows, are merely there to help him along.

This book is there to help him too.

A well-dressed gentleman knows that, once he has left a party, it is not his clothes that will be remembered. Instead, his friends, new and old, will comment on the pleasure of his company and the charm of his conversation. Being a gentleman, those qualities are the essentials of his everyday wardrobe, no matter which suit he pulls out of the closet, no matter which necktie he chooses to go with his shirt.

A gentleman acknowledges and respects life's varying dress codes, but even more, he respects himself.

A gentleman knows that it is *he* who has been invited to the party, not his suit.

A gentleman knows that dressing up may require going to great pains, but he knows that, ultimately, the pain will be forgotten in the fun.

A gentleman knows that looking comfortable is far more important than looking "stylish." After all, style, without comfort, is impossible.

A gentleman understands the importance of first impressions.

A gentleman knows that, for good or ill, he may be making a first impression any time he walks into a room.

A gentleman knows that clothes do not make the man. But he knows that, when making a first impression, his wardrobe may speak louder than his actions—perhaps even louder than his words.

A gentleman knows that his clothes are the first thing others see—before he has a chance to offer a handshake or open his mouth.

If a gentleman is not comfortable in his clothes, he creates discomfort for himself and for those around him.

Confronted with "clever" dress codes, such as "Festive Formal" or "Creative Black Tie," a gentleman has every right to dress as traditionally as he chooses.

If a gentleman is involved in the planning of a social event, he shies away from dress codes such as "Creative Black Tie" or "Black Tie Optional." He thinks back to the times when he was confused about what to wear to an occasion and does not pass that misery on to other gentlemen.

No matter what the trends of fashion, a gentleman knows the colors and cuts in which he looks best.

A gentleman dresses to his strengths.

When shopping for clothes, if a gentleman has to think twice about purchasing a garment—be it a suit, a shirt, or a pair of socks—he is best advised to put it back on the rack.

A gentleman knows that the simple fact that a garment comes in his size is no reason to assume that he is supposed to wear it.

A gentleman remembers that the models in fashion magazines are six foot four and weigh 165 pounds. If he is any shorter than that, or weighs any more, he does not assume that the clothes in the picture were automatically meant for him.

No matter how short he may be, a gentleman stands as tall as he can.

When a gentleman is complimented on his appearance, he accepts the compliment with good grace, saying, "Thank you. It's kind of you to say that."

When he is complimented on his appearance, a gentleman never belittles the compliment by saying, "Gosh, I've had this old jacket since prep school. I'm almost embarrassed to put it on."

Although a gentleman may not dress in the latest style, he dresses neatly, making sure his linen is clean, his shoes are polished, and his socks do not fall down around his ankles.

A gentleman knows that the latest style often is not the greatest style. It may, in fact, have no style at all.

A gentleman feels complimented when he is asked where he shops for his clothes. He does not, however, brag about his designer labels or the price tags that accompanied them.

A gentleman may wear jeans to a semiformal occasion—or even a formal occasion, if he works in the music and entertainment business. But if he chooses to do so, he mixes them with a dark sports coat (ideally a navy or black blazer), a crisply laundered white shirt, and freshly polished black shoes.

If an invitation prescribes a "casual" dress code, a gentleman takes it at its word, wearing jeans (or shorts) and a polo shirt in warm weather or a sweater and slacks in the winter. He adds a sports coat only if he wishes to do so, with full knowledge that he may wish to discard it before the evening is done.

When making a dinner reservation at a fine restaurant (or even at a more casual restaurant), a gentleman always asks, "Do you require that gentlemen wear jackets?" The voice on the other end of the phone may greet him with laughter, but at least he knows that, when he arrives at the front door of the restaurant wearing a polo shirt and slacks, he will not be turned away.

When a gentleman shows up in an open collar and shirtsleeves at a restaurant requiring tie and jacket, he puts on whatever tie and jacket are offered him. Ill-fitting though they may be, he wears them throughout the evening without comment or complaint.

If a gentleman is new to his area and uncertain of the dress code for any particular occasion, he asks his host or hostess for advice, admitting his ignorance—and his desire to make a good impression.

On a formal or even semiformal evening, and whether he is wearing dinner clothes or a dark suit or sports coat, a gentleman is always prepared to remove his jacket to rescue a shivering, bare-shouldered lady.

After requesting that friends wear black tie for an evening at his own home, a gentleman may greet them wearing a smoking jacket, along with the remainder of black-tie regalia.

If a gentleman actually owns a smoking jacket, he runs the risk of being deemed an eccentric by his friends.

No matter what the dress code, a gentleman never attempts to get dressed in a hurry. Inevitably, his fingers will fumble, a button will break, or a zipper will snap. A gentleman has learned that when he allows himself ample time to dress and to care for his appearance, such last-minute difficulties seldom occur.

When a gentleman has accepted the kind invitation to be a groomsman or usher at the wedding of a friend, and when he learns that he may be asked to wear a lime-green, powder-blue, or white tuxedo, he has every right to ask, "Are you *sure?*"

If a gentleman, asked to be a groomsman or usher at the wedding of a friend, learns that accepting that invitation means that he will be required to wear a lime-green, powder-blue, or white tuxedo, he says, "Well, sure. I'm so glad to be asked."

If a gentleman is not absolutely certain as to the dress code for an occasion, he always prefers the risk of being underdressed to that of being overdressed. The former may be interpreted as a simple isunderstanding; the latter suggests conscious premeditation.

A Gentleman from Head to Toe

An Operator's Guide to the Wardrobe Essentials

A gentleman knows that looking good is not just about the grand gesture—the purchase of a trendy designer suit or a pair of obviously Italian-made lace-ups. He knows that, ultimately, being well dressed is about the details—the way he buttons his simple, navy-blue suit jacket or the way he makes sure his penny loafers are always neatly shined.

He knows that, if he pays attention, the drape of his trousers will not be destroyed by pockets made saggy by the burden of car keys, an overstuffed wallet, and a cell phone. He knows that, by taking a moment before rushing out the door in the morning, he can avoid the embarrassment of discovering, shortly before lunchtime, that he's gone halfway through the day wearing mismatched socks. He knows that, with a neatly folded pocket square in his breast pocket and a crisp dimple in his tie, he can declare his personal style without making an issue of the price tag, whether great or small.

A gentleman's ultimate goal is to travel through life as if he were a polished machine and a complete work of art. The following pages offer the advice, instructions, and vocabulary necessary to help him achieve that goal—not only from top to bottom, but also from the inside out.

Hats and Caps

The days are long gone when a hat was a part of a gentleman's everyday existence. Nevertheless, if a gentleman feels comfortable in a hat, be it the familiar fedora to protect him from the chill of winter or a snappy boater to shield him from the heat of the sun, he wears it—recognizing all the while that he is likely to be in the minority these days. He may come off either as an oddity or as the object of universal admiration—the key is the gentleman's own self-confidence and personal style.

A gentleman understands that a hat exists for utilitarian purposes, either to keep him warm or to keep him cool. He understands, therefore, that there is no reason for a hat, or a cap, to be worn inside.

A gentleman may wear his hat or cap in the public areas of any building, other than a house of worship. He understands that public areas include elevators, department stores, and hotel lobbies. He also understands that public areas do not include the reception rooms of doctors' or lawyers' offices or any other place where he expects to engage in one-to-one conversation for any length of time.

If a non-Jewish gentleman accepts an invitation to a Jewish wedding ceremony, funeral, or bar or bat mitzvah, he understands that he may be expected to put on a yarmulke, at least for the time of the ceremony.

If a gentleman has elected to add a hat—a fedora, a Panama, or a boater, for example—to his celebratory getup at a wedding, he removes it inside the house of worship and under the wedding or reception tent. To make life easier for himself while inside the country club or restaurant where the reception is held, he checks his hat at the door.

If a gentleman wears a hat while traveling on a short trip by train or bus, he may choose not to remove it or simply to hold it in his hand. For a longer trip, by train or airplane, however, he will most likely wish to remove his hat, stowing it as carefully as he can in an overhead bin or beneath the seat in front of him.

Unless a gentleman is attending a funeral where men are expected to cover their heads, he removes his hat at any funeral or memorial service. If he attends a graveside service, especially during inclement weather, he may choose to wear his hat, although he understands that he must remove it during any formal prayers.

If a gentleman wears a hat of any kind, even if it is a baseball cap, a stocking cap, or headgear associated with his favorite sports team, he removes it during prayer, during the National Anthem, and during the Pledge of Allegiance.

—

If a gentleman is given to wearing outlandish headgear—such as a plaid deerstalker or a Russian sable cap with earflaps—he understands that he is likely to attract attention.

—

If a gentleman is given to wearing Russian sable caps with earflaps, he may wish to consult a doctor about his need for attention.

—

A GENTLEMAN TIPS HIS HAT

If a gentleman elects to wear a hat, or a cap, he understands what to do with it when greeting others. He "tips" his hat whenever he is being introduced to a new acquaintance or whenever he greets a lady, an older person, or a distinguished personage of either sex. He feels no particular need to tip his hat when greeting another gentleman of approximately his own age and status, although hat tipping always suggests congeniality and respect.

The tradition of tipping one's hat dates from the Middle Ages, when noblemen removed their helmets when greeting one another so as to demonstrate their peaceable intentions and to indicate that they had no fear while in the fellow nobleman's presence. A knight removed his helmet in the presence of a lady, of course, to indicate that he was at her service and that he had no thoughts of seizing her for ransom.

A gentleman understands that "tipping" his

hat no longer means that he must remove it entirely. Instead, he may simply lift his hat quickly from his head and replace it immediately, especially if the wind is chill or if the sun is hot. He may, in fact, simply give the brim of his hat or cap a quick touch, "tipping" it as an indication that he is a man of peace, good will, and good breeding.

HOW TO DETERMINE HAT SIZE

Place one end of a tape measure against your forehead, at the level where your hat will sit. Bring the tape around your head to determine your "head measurement," which then determines your "hat size." Do not attempt to understand the relationship between the two. Simply trust the chart provided herewith:

Head Measurement	Head Size	Hat Size
21⅛"	6¾	S
21½"	6⅞	S
21⅞"	7	M
22¼"	7⅛	M
22⅝"	7¼	L
23"	7⅜	L
23½"	7½	XL
23⅞"	7⅝	XL
24¼"	7¾	2X
24⅝"	7⅞	2X
25"	8	3X

A Gentleman's Glossary: Hats and Caps

boater: A straw hat with a stiff, oval brim and a flat crown.

deerstalker: A soft wool cap of Scottish origins, with visors on both the front and back and earflaps that may be tied up across the head.

derby: A stiff felt hat with a dome-shaped crown and a narrow, curled brim.

fedora: A soft felt hat with a wide, flat brim and the crown creased lengthwise.

homburg: A soft felt hat with a curled brim and the crown creased lengthwise.

Panama: A hat made of soft, easily shaped straw, styled with a wide, flat brim.

top hat (or "stovepipe"): A stiff felt hat with a tall, pipe-shaped crown and flat brim. Its collapsible version is known as an "opera hat."

Haircuts and Grooming

No matter what his budget or his background, when a gentleman heads out for a party or any other public occasion, good grooming is always his first priority. He makes sure that his hair is clean and recently cut. Even if he chooses not to indulge himself in the services of a manicurist, he makes sure that his nails are always clean and freshly trimmed. He shaves carefully and as often as necessary. If he chooses to wear a moustache or beard, he keeps it neatly trimmed. He showers regularly so as to avoid body odor and knows that a good bar of soap is considerably less expensive than a cover-up with heavy cologne. He makes such procedures part of his daily regimen, not saving them for special occasions.

A gentleman owns a pair of tweezers, a set of nail clippers, and a nail file.

Prescription drugs notwithstanding, a gentleman may have little control over that moment when his hairline begins to recede or when his bald spot begins to gleam in the candlelight. He can, however, attempt to keep his wits about him, working with his barber or hairdresser to select a haircut that accentuates his noble bone structure, while drawing attention away from the haircut itself. He washes his hair regularly, using a good shampoo and avoiding heavy pomades and hair dressings. At all costs, he avoids wearing the country-preacher comb-over, which fools nobody and only draws attention to the gentleman's inordinate, and unfortunate, vanity.

A gentleman has no shame in requesting that his barber trim his eyebrows and the hair inside his ears.

While a gentleman avoids any urge to wear heavy makeup, he may still take advantage of skin-care products that help him cope with blemishes, razor burn, and dark circles under his eyes. He also may wish to indulge himself in a good skin toner or the occasional facial scrub, simply because they make him feel better and because he knows that they will pay off, in the long run, by helping him look younger—and feel younger—in ways that cosmetic surgery could never do.

If a gentleman has a dandruff problem, he attempts to correct it by using a medicated shampoo or, if necessary, by consulting his physician. He knows, after all, that black dinner jackets are likely to be a staple of his wardrobe.

A gentleman's barber understands the necessities of a gentleman's social life, sometimes allowing him to schedule last-minute appointments for a trim around the ears.

When a gentleman's barber or stylist does him this sort of favor, a gentleman tips accordingly.

A gentleman has two eyebrows. If he must pluck the hair connecting them, he does so, sipping a bit of Scotch from time to time to dull the pain.

If a gentleman is frequently called upon to attend social events hard on the heels of his workday, he keeps a well-equipped toiletry kit at his office.

If a gentleman thinks of using hair spray, he thinks again.

A gentleman does not try out a new hairstyle on an important occasion—be it a first date, a high-profile society ball, a job interview, or his own wedding.

If a gentleman receives compliments for the smell of his cologne, or the scent of his hair gel, he is wearing too much of a good thing.

A gentleman takes good care of his teeth, brushing them several times daily and flossing regularly. He knows that the gleam of his smile can divert from the shine on his suit.

Unless he is a news anchor or a professional actor, a gentleman does not wear pancake makeup, which is likely to leave unsightly stains on his shirt collar. To make matters worse, it leaves streaks on pillowcases.

A gentleman may, however, treat himself to a facial scrub on a regular basis, just as he may treat himself to a good facial astringent, a soothing aftershave cream, or a cooling eye cream (particularly when he arises after a night of overly gratuitous partying).

If a gentleman plans to attend a social occasion, he schedules an appointment with his barber so that he can make the freshest, neatest appearance possible.

A gentleman washes his face at least once a day, and twice if he is smart.

A gentleman cleans his ears, checking them for wax build-up and leftover shaving cream.

A gentleman clips his nose hairs. At a certain point in his life, well before the end of his forties, he invests in a good-quality electric trimmer for his ears and his nostrils.

A gentleman uses deodorant.

A GENTLEMAN AND HIS COLOGNE

A gentleman considers cologne intimate apparel. It should not cause comment, positive or negative, among other people in the room. Instead, it should be saved as a pleasant surprise for people with whom he makes close physical contact. A gentleman understands that cologne is, after all, an accessory. It is not to be used as a substitute for deodorant. A dab on either side of the neck, with another drop on a gentleman's pocket handkerchief, is quite enough.

When used to excess, cologne is annoying and raises questions about what smells are being covered up. Anytime a person can identify the brand of scent that a man is wearing, he is wearing too much.

A FEW WORDS ABOUT SHAVING

No matter how formal or informal the occasion, if an event occurs on a weeknight, a gentleman is likely to be faced with the ordeal of shaving twice in one day. If a gentleman has sensitive, easily abraded skin, having shaved twice in a day may well lead to a night of torture. Therefore, a gentleman is well advised to think ahead.

If he expects to shave twice in twenty-four hours, he uses a fresh razor (or razor blade) each time he lathers up. He makes sure to moisten his beard thoroughly before shaving and to use plenty of hot water so as to keep his face well steamed throughout the process. If a gentleman is rushed while preparing for a social occasion of any sort, he is well advised to shave *before* showering, in hopes that the steam of his bath will further moisturize his skin and soften any razor-burn abrasions.

Just to make sure, a gentleman is wise to treat his neck to a simple, unscented lotion, followed by a dash of unfussy talcum powder, before buttoning his collar. Later in the evening, while other gentlemen are straining at their collars, he will be grateful for his foresight.

If a gentleman finds that he has nicked himself while shaving, he does not resort to quick fixes, such as styptic pencils. Instead, he takes his time, applying ice cubes and stanching with toilet tissue. He may arrive late at the party, but at least, he will not discover, mid-evening, that his shirt-collar is spackled with gobbets of blood.

And always, just before walking out the door, a gentleman checks his earlobes, just to make sure he is not sporting the dried residue of his shaving cream.

Ties and Other Neckwear

In many high-powered professions, such as law and banking, the necktie remains an everyday fact of life, but even in those professions, it is no longer taken for granted as an obligatory part of the daily dress code. Neckties, however, remain one of the defining factors of the dress codes for many social occasions. (Is it a "black tie" dinner? Is it a "white tie" dance? Even if there's no real "dress code," must I wear a tie to a funeral? Can I get by with a black turtleneck?) Thus, learning which tie to wear and how to tie it—in a variety of knots, remains one of the rituals of training for the gentlemanly life.

A gentleman selects his necktie so that it complements his suit jacket or sports coat.

A gentleman knows that a necktie in a deep red, such as crimson, complements almost any jacket.

A gentleman never wears a necktie that precisely matches his pocket-handkerchief.

A gentleman ties his own bow tie.

Knowing that he will be called upon to tie his own bow tie, a gentleman practices ahead of time—the day or even the week before he expects to get dressed up.

A gentleman ties his standard necktie so that its tip grazes his waistband.

If a gentleman ties his necktie only to discover that two shirt buttons have been left exposed, he ties his tie again.

A gentleman never tucks his over-long necktie into the waistband of his trousers.

A tall or heavy-built gentleman is well advised to purchase extra-long neckties.

A gentleman avoids wearing tie tacks or tie bars, even if they hold sentimental value for him.

A gentleman brushes his teeth *before* putting on his tie—even if it is a bow tie.

When tightening his tie, a gentleman gathers the fabric into *one* simple dimple, to give the knot a finished look and to avoid overly wrinkling the fabric.

When a gentleman washes his hands, he tosses the ends of his necktie behind his neck to avoid spotting them with water.

At all times, but especially on formal occasions, a gentleman is careful not to dribble food on his tie and shirtfront. Nevertheless, except at the most casual gatherings for pizza or pasta, he never tucks his napkin into the neck of his shirt. Instead, he learns not to overload his fork and spoon when transporting messy sauces from table to tongue.

A gentleman is wary of neckties that have hung in his closet the past fifteen years without being worn. A style change of as little as a quarter inch can transform an otherwise beautiful tie into a fashion relic.

Whether his tie is a recent purchase or an old favorite, a gentleman always checks it for food stains and fabric snags.

A gentleman wears an ascot only if he is also wearing a velvet smoking jacket and a pair of embroidered slippers.

If a gentleman chooses to wear an ascot, a velvet smoking jacket, or a pair of embroidered slippers, he pays the price for his decision.

THE CLASSIC KNOTS

WINDSOR KNOT

1. The wide end of the tie should be about a foot below the narrow end. Cross the wide end over the the narrow end.

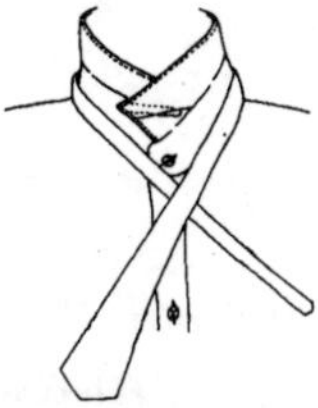

2. Bring the wide end under the narrow end on the right side of your neck.

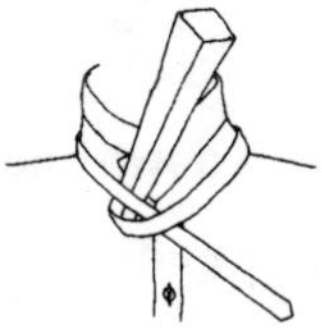

3. Bring the wide end over and let it hang down the front of your shirt.

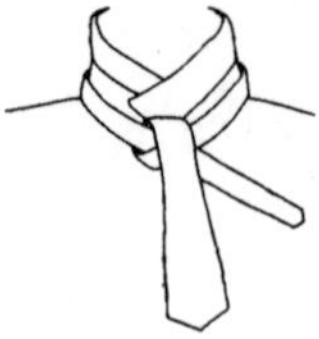

4. Bring the wide end under the remaining narrow end.

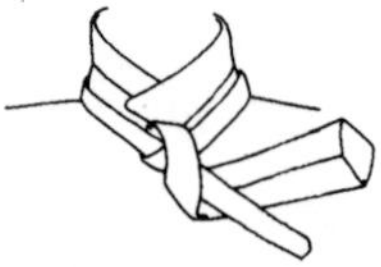

5. Bring the wide end over the working knot and under the narrow part on the right side of your neck.

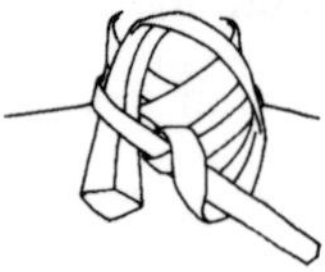

6. Pull the wide end down and cross it over the remaining narrow end.

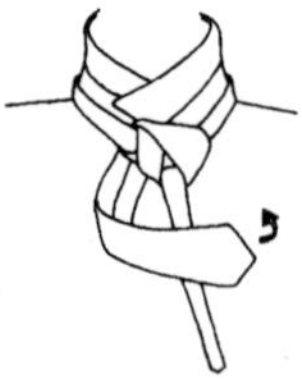

7. Bring the wide end under the narrow part of the tie on the left side of your neck.

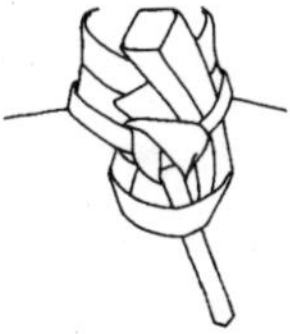

8. Bring the wide end of the tie through the knot that has been created.

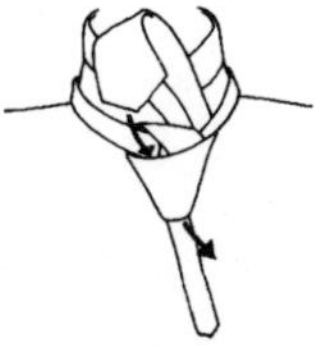

9. Pull the wide end of the tie down the front of your shirt.

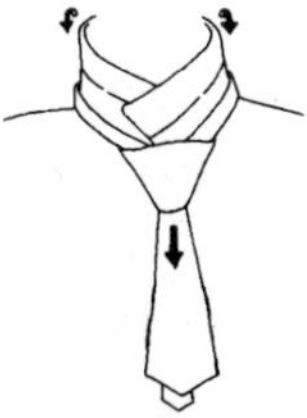

10. Tighten the knot and draw it snug to your collar.

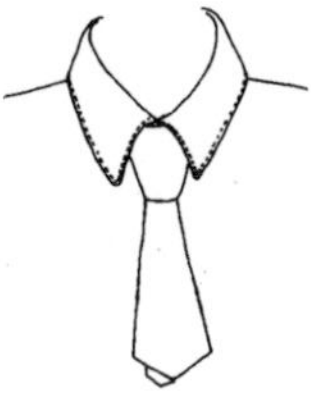

Half Windsor Knot

1. The wide end of the tie should be about a foot below the narrow end. Cross the wide end over the narrow end.

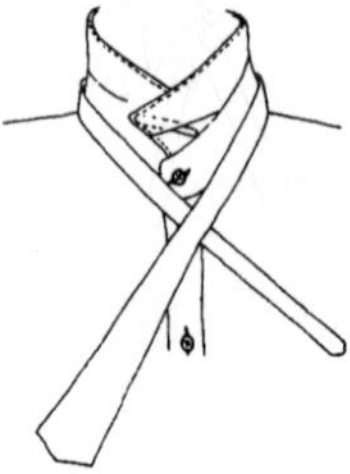

2. Bring the wide end of the tie under the the narrow end.

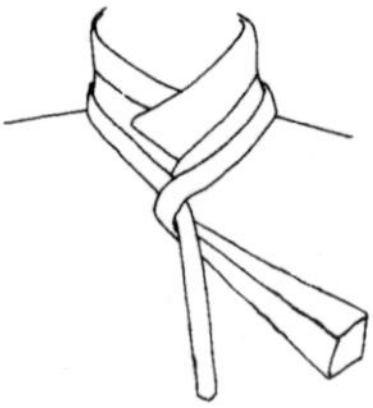

3. Bring the wide end over the narrow end near your neck and under the narrow end on the right side of your neck.

4. Bring the wide end of the tie across your shoulder.

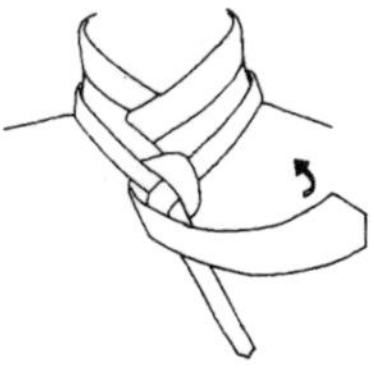

5. Bring the wide of the tie through the knot that has been created.

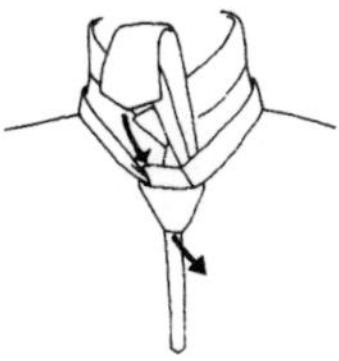

6. Slip the wide end of the tie through the knot completely and down the front of your shirt.

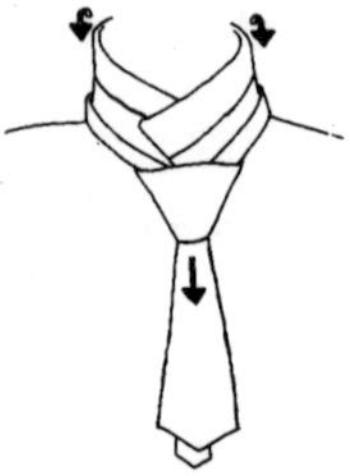

7. Tighten the knot and draw it snug to your collar.

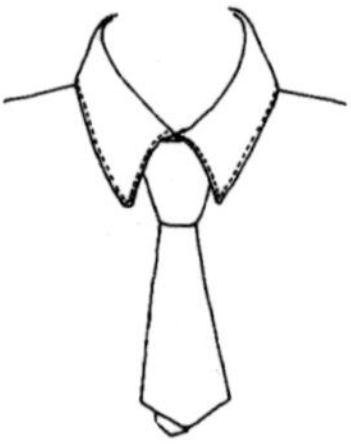

Four-in-Hand Knot

1. The wide end of the tie should be about a foot below the narrow end. Cross the wide end over the narrow end.

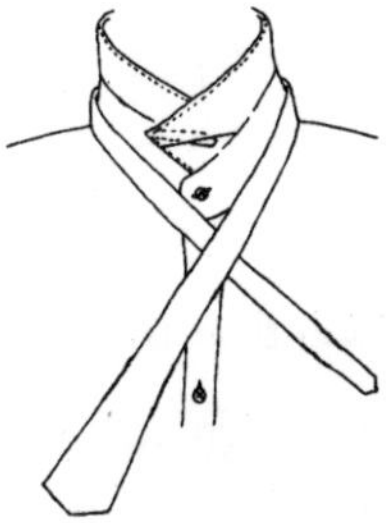

2. Bring the wide end under and then over the narrow end.

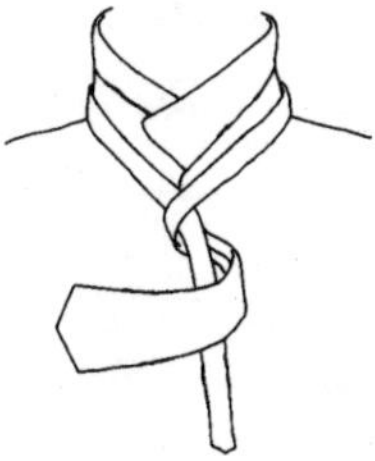

3. Bring the wide end under the narrow part of the tie on the right side of your neck.

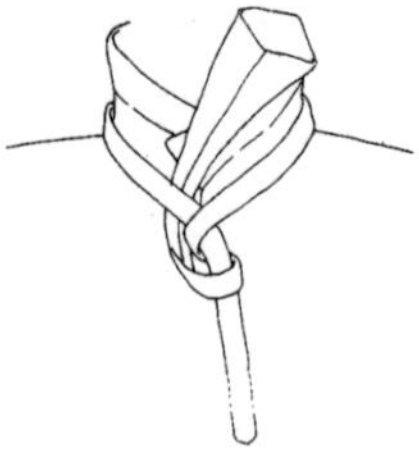

4. Bring the wide end of the tie through the knot that has been created.

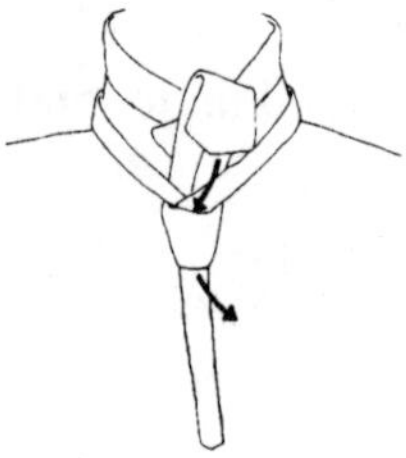

5. Pull the wide end of the tie down the front of your shirt.

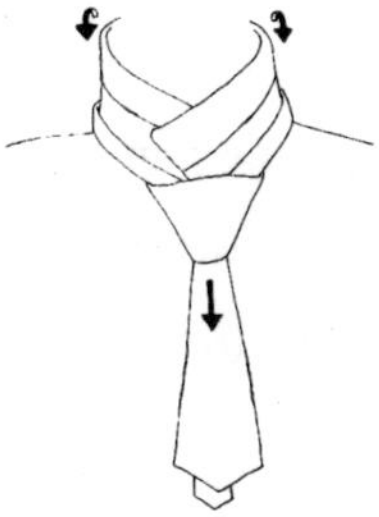

6. Tighten the knot and draw it snug to your collar.

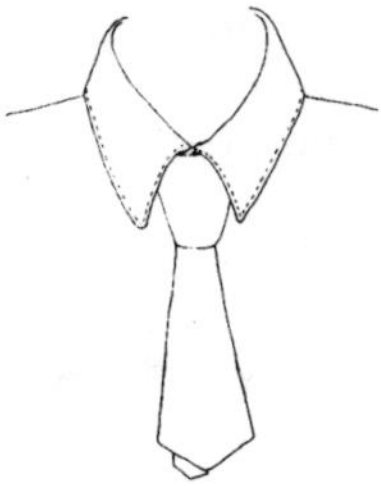

HOW TO TIE A BOW TIE

Tying a bow tie is, essentially, like tying any other bow. A gentleman knows this, and he does not become frustrated if he fumbles the first few times he attempts the procedure. Instead, he gives himself enough practice at home when he does not have a pressing dinner date.

1. Adjust the length of the tie. (A shorter tie will result in a smaller bow. If the tie is left long, the end product has a fluffier, less-tailored look.)

2. Put the tie around your neck. Leave one end hanging longer than the other.

3. Bring the long end of the tie over the short end. Then pull it up from behind, just as if you were beginning a granny knot.

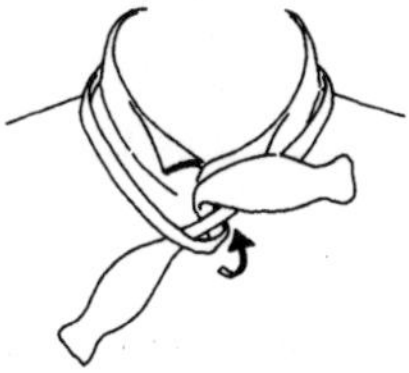

4. Tug securely on both ends.

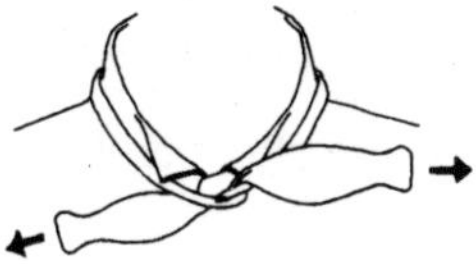

5. Fold the short end of the tie over to make a loop.

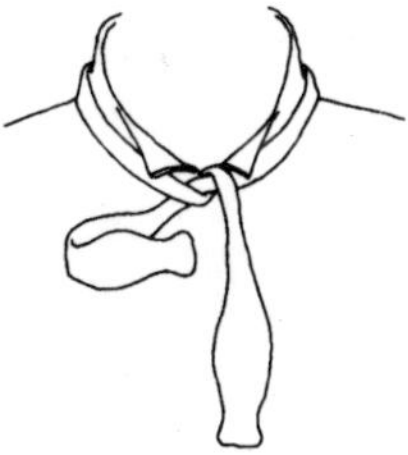

6. Bring the long end of the tie up, over, and around the middle of the entire package.

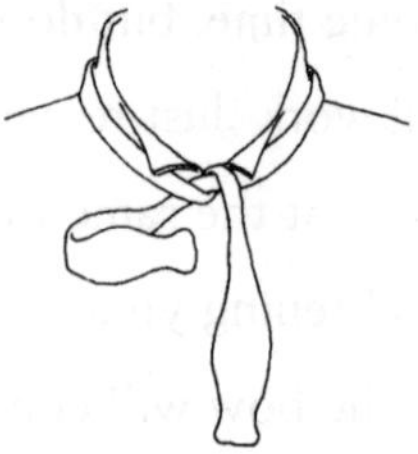

7. Fold the remaining part of the long end into a loop and stuff it through the opening behind the short end. (The loop of the long end must end up behind the flat part of the short end.)

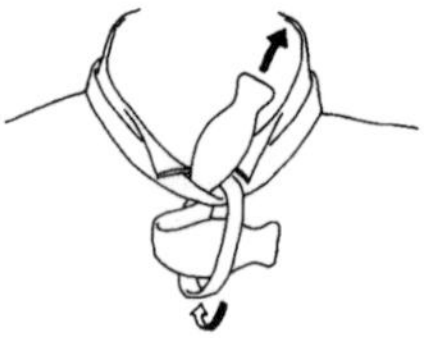

8. Tug on the tie and twist it about until it takes on a neatly finished look. (This step may take some time, but do not give up. It really will work. Just remember to tug on both loops at the same time, just as if you were tightening your shoelaces. Otherwise, the bow will come undone.)

A Gentleman's Glossary: Ties and Other Neckwear

ascot: A scarf, usually silk, worn loosely knotted around the neck and tucked behind a gentleman's shirtfront.

club tie: A necktie patterned with club logos, pseudo-heraldic shields, sports equipment, or any other device indicating a gentleman's allegiance to his club or his favorite pastime.

foulard: A soft silk fabric, woven in tiny twill, usually patterned with abstract floral designs against a solid background. Also, a necktie made from foulard silk.

regimental: A necktie patterned in bright stripes, properly those of the wearer's own military unit. (See "repp" below.)

repp: A stiff-bodied silk fabric, woven in a twill, usually patterned in brightly striped colors. Also, a necktie made from repp silk; sometimes used interchangeably with "regimental."

SHIRTS, COLLARS, AND CUFFS

Whether it is the crisply laundered shirt he puts on for a job interview, the polo shirt he wears at the office, the wing-collar formal shirt he brings out only for weddings, or the T-shirt he pulls on to run errands on Saturday, a gentleman's shirt is the defining item of his wardrobe. Even in the most stuffy work environment, a gentleman is likely to spend most of his day in his shirtsleeves, covering it with his jacket only when he heads to outside appointments or to the conference table. Whatever the dress code in his everyday life, however, a gentleman knows that when he chooses a shirt, he is also choosing a frame for his face. He selects it carefully, in terms of color, pattern, and fit, sticking with a look that suits him even if it means he wears the same style shirt every day. When even the best-loved shirt has grown worse for wear, however, a gentleman lets it go. Stains, broken buttons, and frayed cuffs can detract from even the best-rehearsed sales pitch—or the most heartfelt protestation of love.

If a gentleman does not have a tapered physique, he does not attempt to wear tapered shirts.

If a gentleman discovers, when he sits down, that the buttons on his shirtfront are straining against the fabric, he moves to a larger shirt size.

If a gentleman finds it a struggle to button his collar, he moves to a more comfortable fit.

When trying on a shirt, a gentleman tests the fit, both sitting and standing.

If a gentleman is thick-set, he avoids spread collars.

When hard at work in his private office, in the office pool, or in the newsroom, a gentleman may unbutton his collar button and loosen his tie. When he hits the streets for lunch or a business appointment, however, he rebuttons and retightens.

If a gentleman wears French cuffs, he selects simple cufflinks for the office or for any occasion that calls for a business suit.

A gentleman knows that "simple cufflinks" are made of classic metals, such as gold, silver, or platinum, with settings of enamel or semiprecious stones.

A gentleman knows that tasteful engraving does not destroy the simplicity of cufflinks.

A gentleman saves his glittery cufflinks, especially those set with precious stones, for formal evening wear.

A gentleman saves his amusing cufflinks, especially the ones that light up in the dark, for New Year's Eve.

When dressing for a formal occasion, a gentleman's cufflinks need not match his shirt studs precisely. The links and studs should, however, complement each other.

A gentleman does not wear a short-sleeved shirt with a suit.

A gentleman knows that the term "short-sleeved dress shirt" is an oxymoron.

A gentleman's shirt cuffs extend approximately a half-inch from the sleeves of his jacket, but a gentleman's cufflinks never actually show unless the gentleman is extending his hand or bending his elbow.

During any meal, a gentleman takes care to keep his shirtfront clean. If food should splatter on his clean shirt, he excuses himself and does the best he can to remedy the situation with a little soda water from the bar or some warm tap water from the men's room.

If a gentleman's shirt becomes soiled and no replacement shirt is handy, he does not call attention to the mess.

If a gentleman's shirt becomes stained or faded due to his choice of deodorant, he tosses out the shirt and changes to another deodorant.

—

A gentleman may think he sweats so little that he can ask for "no starch" at the laundry. Especially if he lives in the South, that gentleman is wrong.

—

A gentleman is not ashamed to ask his laundry to turn the collars of his good dress shirts, so that he can enjoy them for at least a few more wearings.

—

Once a shirt's collars and cuffs are irreparably frayed and its color has grown dingy, a gentleman acknowledges the fact and wears it only for Saturday chores and errands.

—

THE CLASSIC COLLARS

Button Collar

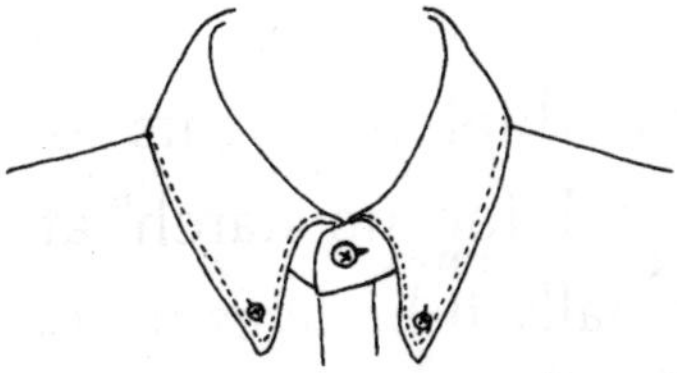

Rounded (or "French") Collar

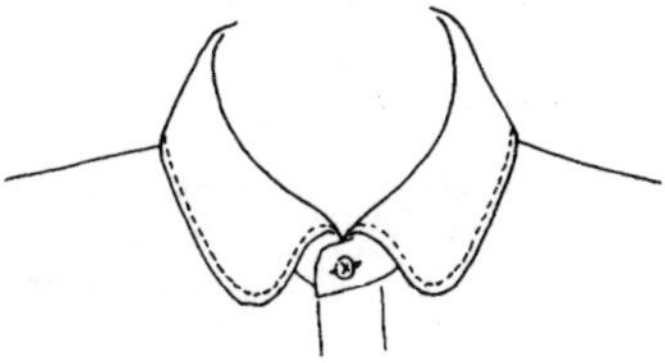

Spread Collar

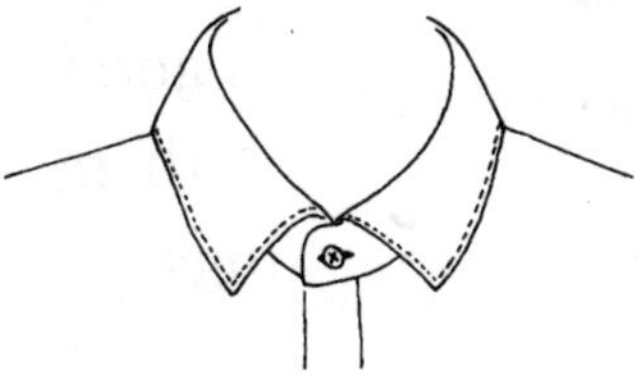

Wing Collar

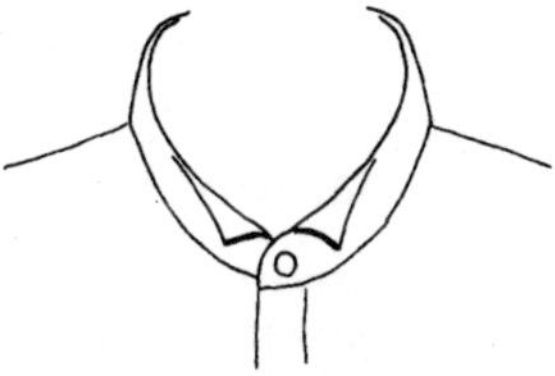

Straight Collar

A WORD ABOUT THE BUTTON-DOWN COLLAR

The button-down collar was introduced to America by Brooks Brothers, Inc., shortly after the turn of the twentieth century. The style was derived from South American soccer players who buttoned the points of their collars down to their jerseys to discourage the collar points from slapping them in the face.

The American business community adopted the style wholeheartedly, with little regard for its origin. At this time, major politicians, business executives, and serious academicians all seem to have adopted the button-down as collar of choice, at least for daytime appointments and appearances.

Nevertheless, the fact is that the button-down collar remains considerably less formal than a straight collar. For example, a gentleman may substitute a plain, straight-collar shirt for an exclusively "formal" shirt if he finds that he must make a last-minute appearance at a black-tie dinner. But he resorts to a white button-down only if it is the last alternative remaining in his shirt closet.

When a gentleman requires a dress shirt, but wishes to go tie-less, a button-down is almost always his best alternative. But if the occasion begins after five o'clock in the evening and a gentleman feels the urge to wear a tie, he leaves his button-down at home and prefers a button-less model.

A Gentleman's Glossary: Shirts, Collars, and Cuffs

barrel cuff: The style of cuff standard on most American-made dress shirts, consisting of a band of fabric fastened around the wrist with a button.

French cuff: A style of cuff consisting of a double fold of fabric, fastened around the wrist with a cuff link.

oxford cloth: A longwearing cotton fabric, woven in a tight basket weave, often used for daytime dress shirts.

pinpoint oxford: A smooth-surfaced cotton fabric, tightly woven with light thread, often used for fine business and formal shirts.

TROUSERS

A gentleman knows that, just as with blazers and jackets, some trousers are true classics. A pair of superbly cut gray flannels will serve him humbly and well. Some gentlemen may attempt to fool themselves into thinking that their trousers are somehow subordinate, in every sense of the word, since they are hidden by a jacket. But a wise gentleman knows that, at some point in the day, even at a high-powered business conference, he may wish to remove his jacket, roll up his sleeves, and get down to work. He also knows that, at some point on a brisk evening, he may wish to share his jacket with a shivering lady friend. He knows that when such moments arise, he, his shirt, and his pants are left alone to face the world. He is wise if he has visited his tailor, and his dry cleaner, before he faces those moments.

A gentleman knows that the terms "trousers" and "pants" may be used interchangeably.

A gentleman uses the term "slacks" to refer to trousers not intended to be worn as part of a suit.

A gentleman knows that if his suit jacket is a bit snug, he can unbutton it. He knows, however, that if his pants are too tight, he has no such option.

Unless a gentleman is absolutely certain that his stomach will not spill over his waistband, he avoids any temptation toward beltless trousers.

When searching for a pair of trousers, a gentleman does not lie about his waist size—neither to himself nor to the sales clerk.

A gentleman follows the guidance of a trusted sales clerk, who understands that one designer's size 34 trousers may be another designer's size 36.

A gentleman remembers the same realities when purchasing trousers over the Internet.

When a gentleman stands, his pants are long enough to cover his socks.

A gentleman's trouser cuffs fall into a slight "break" around his ankles and over the tops of his shoes.

A gentleman shops for his trousers at an establishment known for its tailoring services.

A gentleman knows that only a good tailor understands how to guarantee the proper "break" in his trousers and a smooth fit across his rear end.

A gentleman's suit pants, and any trousers he intends to wear with a jacket or to even the most vaguely formal occasion, are always cuffed.

A gentleman may choose to add cuffs to any of his trousers, except for his jeans and the trousers of his formalwear.

A gentleman sees that the cuffs of his trousers are no deeper than one and one-quarter inch.

A gentleman stands tall while having his trousers fitted.

A gentleman saves the extra buttons that come with his new trousers, knowing that he will need them to replace the buttons invariably ripped from his back pockets.

When planning to have a new pair of trousers fitted, a gentleman wears the style of underwear he most commonly wears.

A gentleman may wish to have his trousers fitted with both belt loops and suspender buttons, but he never makes use of both at the same time.

A gentleman does not fill his pants pockets with unnecessary paraphernalia.

A gentleman knows that a bulky key ring, a wallet stuffed with credit cards, or a cell phone can destroy the line of even the most beautifully cut pair of trousers.

A gentleman does not wear white trousers, nor the white shoes that match them, until after Memorial Day.

A gentleman puts away his white trousers after Labor Day.

A Gentleman's Glossary: Trousers

belt fob: A small loop of fabric set into the waistband of a pair of trousers, positioned so that the tongue of a gentleman's belt can pass through it to assist in holding his trousers in place.

break: An allowance of fabric provided at the hem of a gentleman's trousers, covering his socks and the tops of his shoelaces when he stands.

change pocket: A small pocket set into the pocket lining of a pair of trousers.

hand: The texture or feel of a fabric, used most often in reference to fabric used for trousers.

watch pocket: A small pocket, flapped or unflapped, set into the waistband of a pair of trousers.

Suits, Blazers, and Sports Coats

Even if a gentleman does not wear a suit to the office, he knows he does not live a suit-free life. Inevitably, he will be called upon to dress for one of life's special occasions. He keeps a suit—cut in a timeless style and made in a timeless color (navy, black, or gray)—on the ready at all times. What's more, if he is not called upon to wear his all-purpose suit with great regularity, he tries it on, from time to time, to make sure the buttons actually button around his waist. A gentleman also equips himself with at least one classic sports coat. A good tweed or camel-hair jacket will carry him through almost any fall or winter event, but the best friend in his entire wardrobe is likely to be a navy-blue blazer, made of a year-round-weight worsted wool. Such a jacket is a gentleman's ally in all seasons of the year and in all hours of the day.

When a gentleman wears a double-breasted suit, he never leaves the jacket unbuttoned—not even just one of the buttons—at least while he is standing.

When a gentleman finds that his suit jacket no longer buttons comfortably, he does not play games with himself. He either has it altered or sends it to a charity thrift shop.

A gentleman knows that a more expensive suit may be well worth the money, if only because it allows more excess fabric in the seams to accommodate the comings and goings of his waistline.

If a gentleman owns only one suit, it is navy, black, or gray.

If a gentleman can afford only one fine suit, rather than three inferior ones, no matter how good the deal sounds in the newspaper, he goes for the finer option.

If a gentleman owns only one good suit, he is proud to wear it often, since it never raises questions as to cut, color, and style.

If a gentleman owns only one suit, it is made of worsted wool.

If it is well cut, the jacket of a gentleman's dark suit may also serve him as a sports coat.

If a gentleman's backside is of any considerable volume and if that gentleman purchases a ventless jacket, he makes sure that the jacket is more than ample of cut.

A gentleman carries as few items as possible in the pockets of his trousers, thereby preserving their handsome drape and saving wear and tear on the pocket linings.

A gentleman never puts his hands in his jacket pockets. To the best of his ability, he keeps his hands out of his trouser pockets, as well.

Although a gentleman's jacket may come equipped with four front buttons, he feels no necessity to button them all.

Unless he is extremely slender and of a considerable height, a gentleman is most often wise to button only one of his jacket buttons.

—

A gentleman's jacket sleeves are short enough to display a half-inch of his shirt cuffs.

—

A gentleman feels comfortable wearing a good, dark suit to any occasion that does not demand formalwear.

—

A gentleman feels comfortable wearing a classic blazer, worn with simple gray trousers, to any occasion where a business suit would be accepted.

—

A gentleman's vest is long enough to cover the waistband of his trousers.

A gentleman leaves the bottom button of his vest unbuttoned, no matter what the time of day.

The pants legs of a gentleman's suit are always cuffed, unless they are part of his formalwear.

A gentleman never wears cuffs on his formal trousers.

If a gentleman owns even one suit or sports coat, he knows the phone number of a good tailor.

A TRIBUTE TO THE NAVY BLAZER

A gentleman in a navy-blue blazer sails through life with utter self-confidence. More than any other jacket in the world of wardrobe, the navy blazer has earned its right of admission to virtually any event that does not require black tie and patent-leather shoes. Its origins are in the world of sailing, and it carries with it the snappy air of the ship's captain and the debonair style of a kingly yachtsman. Its brass buttons, a relic of its military past, come in handy for catching the eye of an attractive stranger—or a negligent cocktail server. If the style of the blazer is double-breasted, the v-pattern created by the buttons may even help suggest that the gentleman's chest is indeed somewhat wider than his waist.

If it is cut from good worsted wool, a navy blazer can travel in all climates and in all seasons. In the fall and winter, it seems drawn to a pair of gray flannel trousers, while in springtime and summer, it is perfectly set off by a pair of light grays, colorful cottons, or even white linens (but only if the weather is very fine). If a gentleman's wardrobe can be said to have an actual "staple" (in the same way that a lady's wardrobe can be based on one little black dress), it is his blazer. For many a gentleman, it is the first jacket ever bought for him by his parents. It may be replaced by many another blazer almost exactly like it, but the relationship remains the same forever—confident, unpretentious, and unwavering.

A Gentleman's Glossary: Suits, Blazers, and Sports Coats

blazer: A nautically inspired jacket, single- or double-breasted, with peaked or notched lapels and brass buttons, usually engraved or embossed with a monogram or insignia. Its classic color is navy blue.

camel hair: A soft-textured fabric, woven from the actual hair of camels, sometimes blended with other fibers, often used for men's sports coats and overcoats.

cashmere: An extremely soft fine wool, shorn from goats, often used for fine sports coats, blazers, and overcoats.

drape: The manner in which a gentleman's well-fitted jacket or trousers literally "hang" on his body.

drop: The difference, in standard suit sizes, between a gentleman's jacket size and his waist size. For most off-the-rack suits, that difference is six sizes. For example, a size-46 suit usually consists of a size-46 jacket and size-40 pants.

fusing: A method using heat, pressure, and adhesive to bond layers of fabric so as to reduce the actual amount of sewing. Only a few of the finest custom-made suits are still constructed with absolutely no fused seams.

sports coat: A short, buttoned jacket, of any style, not intended to serve as part of a suit.

tweed: A richly textured fabric, in wool or other fabrics, characterized by a mixture of patterns and colors.

worsted: A smooth wool fabric, woven in a tiny twill pattern, often used for suits and jackets intended for year-round wear.

Formalwear

Although the term "informal" was coined to indicate that gentlemen were expected to show up wearing black tie, rather than "formal" clothing (white-tie bib-and-tucker), an "informal" dress code now usually demands a sports coat and tie or, at the very stuffiest, a business suit. Nevertheless, many a gentleman lives in fear of the moment when a black-tie invitation—or, God help him, a white-tie invitation—will arrive in the mail. The prospect of that moment, however, should actually fill him with calm, since a request for black tie leaves little margin for error. Even in today's ever-evolving, constantly adapting society, the formula for formalwear remains virtually unchanged. The suit remains black, as do the tie and shoes that go with it. If a gentleman expects formal evenings to be even an occasional part of his life, he may choose to purchase his own suit. Meanwhile, rental remains a perfectly acceptable option, whether the gentleman is headed to the highest of society weddings or the dressiest ball following a presidential inauguration.

A gentleman realizes that purchasing his own formalwear is a sizable investment—and a longtime commitment. Thus, when considering this momentous step, he shops in a respected men's store.

When a gentleman purchases his own formalwear, he buys a suit that fits him comfortably or even loosely (within reason). He knows that dress-up parties involve rich food and ample drink. He also knows that they occur at all times of the year, during none of which he wishes to feel too large for his trousers.

When his dinner clothes are fitted, a gentleman makes sure that ample fabric remains in the seams, in anticipation of the potential expansion of his waistline.

A gentleman knows that a formal shirt does not have a button-down collar.

If a gentleman elects to wear a wing collar, he wears his collar points *behind* his bow tie.

When shopping for dinner clothes, a gentleman steers away from "blended" fabrics. He searches, instead, for light worsted wool, which is cooler in the summer and which sheds wrinkles more easily than other "easy-care" fabrics.

When a gentleman wears a cummerbund, he makes sure the pleats are turned upward, forming little pockets in which he may stash a theater ticket or a calling card—his own or, perhaps, someone else's.

If a gentleman tends toward fleshiness, he thinks twice before wearing a wing collar.

If a gentleman expects to be invited to black-tie occasions on a regular basis, he goes ahead and buys his own suit and accessories. After three or four wearings, that initial investment can easily justify itself, given the cost—and quality—of rented formal clothes.

When a gentleman wears a formal vest—or any vest, for that matter—he leaves at least one bottom button unbuttoned. If a second unbuttoned button makes him feel more comfortable (and if he is tall enough to bring it off), he indulges himself in that way too.

A gentleman will do well to remember that in England (where the concept of black suits for gentleman, as evening wear, was born), a "vest" is an undergarment (known as a "tank top" in the U.S.). The sleeveless, buttoned-up garment worn between coat and shirtfront is more properly known as a "waistcoat" (pronounced "weskit," if a gentleman affects a British accent, although a gentleman *never* affects a British accent).

A gentleman may wish to add a dash of color to a summertime formal party by wearing a colorful dinner jacket. When doing so, however, he realizes that he also runs the risk of looking like a member of a band conducted in 1947 by Xavier Cugat. Or worse yet, a band conducted in 1953 by Desi Arnaz.

If a gentleman feels the urge to wear a colorful cummerbund, tie, or pocket square, he does not buy them as a "set." A gentleman's pocket square, tie, and cummerbund were never intended to share the same gene pool.

If a gentleman is the groom at a wedding, his dinner clothes or evening clothes differ in no way from those of the other members of the wedding party—or even from those worn by the wedding guests. He may wear a boutonniere, taken from the bride's bouquet, but otherwise he sticks to the standard uniform.

A gentleman knows that, when mixing blue jeans with a dinner jacket, he runs the risk of suggesting that only half his suit was returned from the dry cleaners.

A gentleman makes sure that his dinner clothes are always clean and unwrinkled, lest he require them at a moment's notice.

Unless he is an attendant at a nighttime wedding party, invited to a formal ball, or tapped to receive a Nobel Prize, it is highly likely that a gentleman will never be faced with the necessity of being fitted for a tailcoat.

If a gentleman receives an invitation marked "Black Tie Optional," he knows that black tie is what his host or hostess really wants him to wear—but the choice to do so is his own.

A gentleman knows that white dinner jackets were invented to be worn only in tropical climes—and on movie sets. There is seldom any good excuse for wearing such a jacket north of the South Carolina state line.

There is *no* good excuse for wearing a white dinner jacket, anywhere, between Labor Day and Memorial Day.

If, at a summertime black-tie dinner, the announcement is made that "gentlemen may remove their jackets," an experienced gentleman considers his options: He may remove his jacket and catch a bit of the breeze. Or he may decline the offer, knowing that underneath his jacket, a sweat-soaked shirt now clings to his torso. Being a gentleman, he may choose *not* to share that reality with his fellow dinner guests.

RENTING FORMALWEAR

If a gentleman is only rarely invited to black-tie affairs, he may find it more convenient to rent his formalwear. When he rents black tie, however, he undertakes the mission as seriously as if he were purchasing the suit for long-term wear. On such occasions, he is wise to observe the following precautions:

1. Plan ahead. A gentleman does not wait until the last moment to handle such a serious matter. He consults friends as to the reputations of various rental establishments, perhaps even visiting the stores to ask about their rental fees, rental-return policies, and the time required for the suit to be tailored after the fitting. (A gentleman never assumes that he might simply stroll in and out of the store with a suit casually picked from the rack.)

2. Choose black. Nothing else works. Nothing else is right. Nothing else need be said.

3. Pick it up early. A wise gentleman picks up his rental finery at least two days before the event, giving himself plenty of time to try on the jacket and trousers to make sure they have been altered according to plan.

4. Try it on, then and there. An even wiser gentleman tries on his suit before ever leaving the store. He also checks to be sure all accessories, including cufflinks and studs, shoes, and cummerbund, are in order.

5. Turn it in on time. A wise gentleman makes sure he is aware of the return deadline, to avoid extra costs and unpleasant surprises.

6. Consider buying it. Most quality rental establishments also sell formalwear. Many such establishments mount annual sales at which lightly used suits may be purchased at greatly reduced prices.

THE OTHER BLACK TIE

A gentleman may not own his own dinner clothes, and he may not wish to rent them, considering the cost of leasing a dinner jacket for a single evening, much less a weekend.

Instead, a gentleman may wish to invest in a good-quality black or midnight-blue suit, cut in an understated, classic style (that is, a style that does not involve top-stitching on the jacket or velveteen insets on the trouser legs). Absolutely appropriate for weddings, funerals, and romantic dinners, such a suit will also carry him through almost any semiformal occasion ("semiformal" being a euphemism for "black tie"). When wearing this suit, on this sort of occasion, he adds to it a simple white dress shirt with a straight collar, an elegant tie in a solid color (a silk crepe in black, dark blue, or silver works well), and freshly polished smooth-leather shoes, along with dark, solid socks.

This sort of outfit, in fact, is usually a far

superior choice to a poorly fitted rental tux. A gentleman in a good suit that fits him is always more comfortable than a fellow in a suit he has merely borrowed.

THE FORMAL OPTIONS

Morning Coat

Tailcoat

Dinner Jacket

A Gentleman's Glossary: Formalwear

black tie: A suit consisting of a black wool jacket with black satin lapels and matching trousers with a black satin stripe down the outside of the pants leg. Traditionally worn with a black satin bow tie and waistcoat or cummerbund to match. Formally known as "dinner clothes." See "tuxedo."

cummerbund: A wide, pleated sash worn around a gentleman's waistband as part of formalwear.

dinner jacket: A short coat, worn on formal occasions, usually tailored of solid-black worsted wool with either a shawl collar, notched lapels, or peaked lapels in dull black satin. Dinner jackets tailored in cream or off-white worsted are sometimes seen in the southern United States or in resort areas, during the summer months. No matter what the jacket's color, it is traditionally worn with black worsted wool trousers ornamented by a black satin stripe running up the outside of the pants legs. Together, the dinner jacket and its trousers are known as "dinner clothes" or, more colloquially, as a "tuxedo."

morning suit: A suit consisting of gray morning coat and striped trousers, the daytime equivalent of white tie, usually seen at only the most formal pre-noon weddings.

soft collar: A formal shirt with a straight point collar, similar to a daytime business dress shirt.

stroller (or "boulevard"): A suit consisting of a short gray coat and striped or light gray trousers, usually seen at extremely formal afternoon weddings.

studs: Removable decorative buttons, sometimes made with precious metals or gems, worn with a gentleman's formal shirt.

tailcoat: A formal coat with black satin lapels. The coat is cut short in the front, but long in back, with gently curved "tails" reaching to the break in the gentleman's knee.

tuxedo: Colloquial for a gentleman's black-tie suit.

waistcoat: The traditional term for a gentleman's formal vest. When shopping for a suit of any kind in Great Britain, a gentleman would never ask for a "vest," a term which, in the British Isles, refers to a sleeveless undershirt.

white tie: A suit consisting of a black wool tailcoat and matching trousers with a black satin stripe down the outside of the pants leg. Traditionally worn with white cotton, linen, or satin bow tie and matching waistcoat.

wing collar: A formal shirt with a band collar, the ends of the band cut in points to resemble "wings."

Shoes

A gentleman may be forgiven for having spilled a bit of soup on his tie at supper. He may be excused for having grown a bit too wide for his summer slacks. But he may never forgive himself for wearing a pair of scuffed shoes—especially if he wears them to a crucial job interview or to a cocktail reception where he intends to make his best impression. In many professions and on many social occasions, black shoes still remain the rule, but whether his shoes are black cap-toe oxfords, cordovan loafers, or patent leather dancing pumps, a gentleman makes sure that they are freshly polished, with the heels and soles in at least reasonably respectable shape. He may not have absolute control over the splashing of his soup or the size of his waistline, but his shoes, he knows, can always be fixed. They are there to carry him, in more ways than one, through the marbled corridors, over the cobblestones, and across the polished dance floors of life.

A gentleman knows that an ill-fitting shoe is always the wrong shoe, no matter what the occasion.

If he can possibly avoid it, a gentleman does not wear a new pair of shoes to an important occasion, especially if they have soles of slick leather.

A gentleman owns at least two pairs of shoes so that he is not forced to wear the same pair two days in a row.

A gentleman attempts never to wear the same pair of shoes two days in a row, for the sake of the shoes, not for the sake of fashion.

If a gentleman hopes to work in the legal or banking profession, he is wise to wear black shoes for his job interview.

If a gentleman is invited to any occasion requesting "business attire" or a more formal dress code, and beginning after six o'clock in the evening, he wears black shoes.

A gentleman never wears wingtips with his dinner clothes.

To complement his formal dress, a gentleman may put on black suede or quilted-velvet evening shoes, but it is ill advised for him to carry such lightheartedness beyond his own front door.

When a gentleman discovers that any of his shoes—whether cap-toe oxfords, penny loafers, formal pumps, or cowboy boots—need new heels or new soles, he takes them to the shop—not only for the good of his social life, but for the good of his shoes.

Unless he makes his living as a cattle rancher or a country singer, a gentleman does not wear cowboy boots with a suit.

Whatever his profession, a gentleman does not attempt to mix his tailored suit with his tennis shoes.

A gentleman keeps at least one extra pair of shoelaces on hand—both at home and at the office—in case of emergencies.

A gentleman polishes his shoes on a regular basis.

A gentleman knows that a professional shoeshine is invariably a solid investment.

HOW TO SHINE A PAIR OF LEATHER SHOES

The necessary equipment: Soft cloth, wax polish, water, soft brush (optional).

The procedure:

1. Sprinkle a bit of warm water over the polish. (And yes, spit works just fine.)
2. Cover a finger with the soft cloth and use it to work the water into the polish.
3. Apply the polish to the shoe.
4. Work the polish into the leather.
5. Using a clean section of the cloth (or a soft brush), buff the leather to a brilliant shine.

A GUIDE TO FOOTWEAR

Loafer

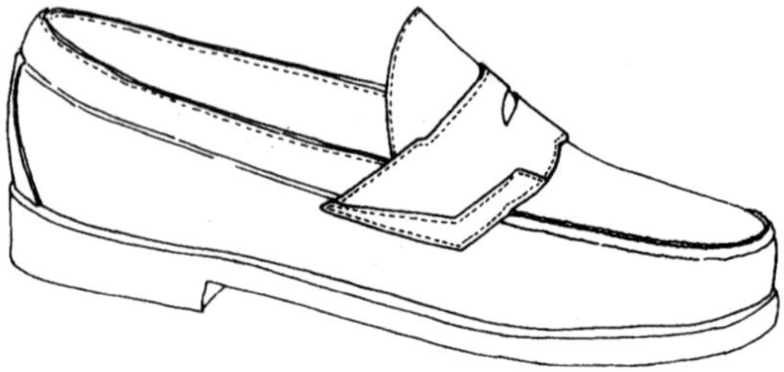

Monkstrap

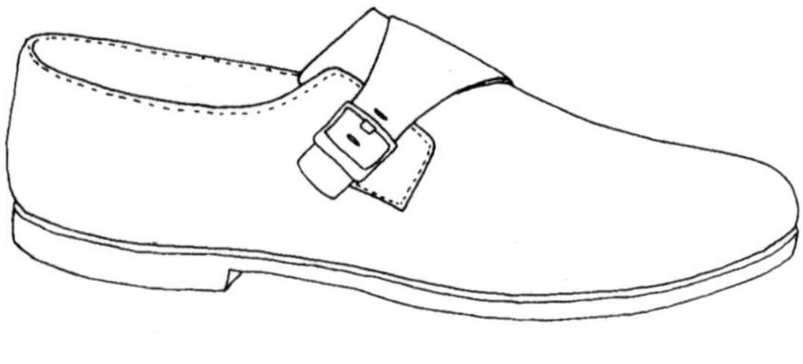

Tassel Slip-on

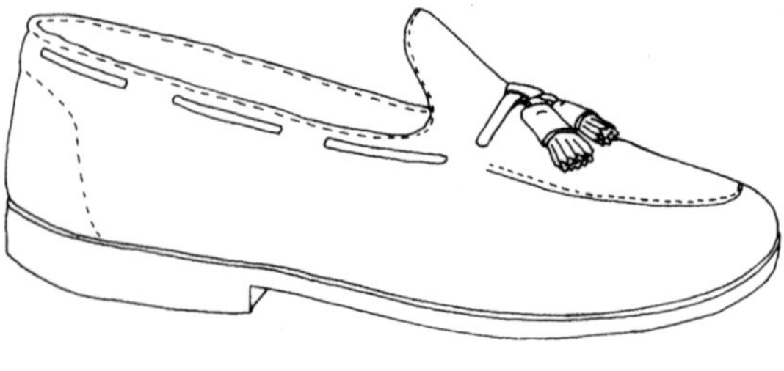

Cap-Toe Oxford

Wingtip

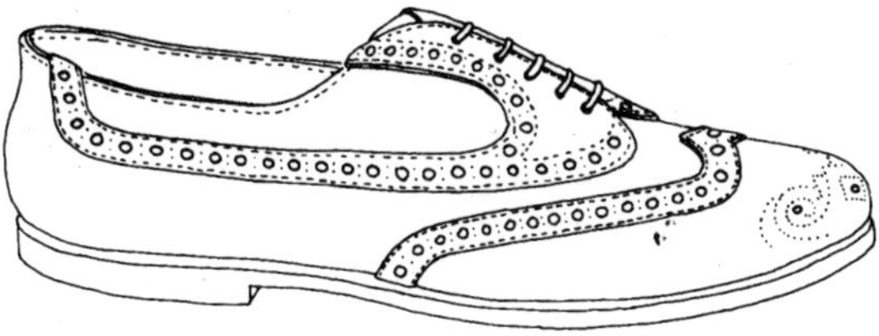

Formal Pump

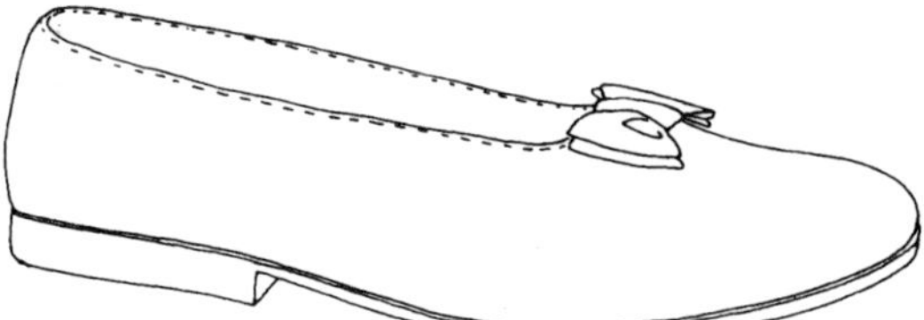

THE FITTING SHOE

A gentleman selects his footwear as follows:

The Outfit	The Shoes
Black/navy business suit	Black lace-ups or slip-ons
Gray business suit	Black, brown, or cordovan lace-ups or slip-ons
Brown or tan suit	Brown or cordovan slip-ons or loafers
Blue blazer and flannels	Black, brown, or gray cordovan slip-ons or loafers
Black tie	Black patent leather pumps or lace-ups
White tie	Black patent leather pumps

A Gentleman's Glossary: Shoes

benchmade: Adjective describing a shoe on which at least 25 percent of the work was done by hand.

bespoke: Adjective describing a shoe entirely made to order.

cap-toe oxford: A lace-up shoe, ornamented with a line of stitching across the toe, appropriate for business or social wear.

cordovan: A fine, dark-red leather, made of split cowhide, but originally from the hides of goats from Cordoba, Spain.

kiltie: A shoe with an ornamental fringe of slashed leather covering the instep of a loafer or other slip-on shoe.

loafer: A casual slip-on shoe, the top of the shoe stitched to the shoe's body, moccasin-style.

monkstrap: A plain-toed shoe, with a buckle strap over the instep.

oxford: A plain-toed lace-up shoe.

pump: A formal shoe with a very low vamp, exposing most of the instep.

wingtip: A lace-up shoe with a layer of scallop-cut, perforated leather added for ornamentation at the toe.

The Finishing Touches

Socks and Underwear
Belts and Suspenders
Gloves, Scarves, and Overcoats
And All the Rest

A gentleman is not just a man of broad gestures. He is also a man of detail. His appearance is not meant to create a fuss. A gentleman knows that underneath it all, while he is holding the limelight with his witty conversation or his trenchant analysis of recent politics, the most seemingly insignificant of his accessories may steal away a listener's attention, for good or for ill. He dresses well, not just from sole to crown, but from the inside out.

For any number of reasons, a gentleman owns several pairs of nylon, silk, nylon-and-silk, cashmere, or nylon-and-wool black socks—all of which he is confident will *not* bunch down around his ankles during the course of a dinner party.

A gentleman chooses his socks-of-the-day so that they blend with his slacks or his suit pants—not so that they match his shirt or tie, much less his pocket square.

In hopes of adding a dash of color to his wardrobe, a gentleman may choose to wear brightly colored socks with his dinner clothes. If so, he makes sure that the break in his pants legs is sufficient to keep his little touch of excitement undercover, at least while he is standing.

If a gentleman is of an athletic build or is taller than five foot four, he buys his socks in an over-the-calf length. Otherwise, in order to prevent a display of white ankle above sagging socks, his only option is to resort to sock garters, which may still be purchased although their heyday was the 1930s, when gentlemen apparently had no concern for the flow of blood to their calves and feet.

Even if a gentleman does not anticipate being in an automobile accident, he remembers his mother's advice and wears clean underwear and hole-free socks whenever he leaves the house.

A gentleman wears an undershirt, especially if he is given to profuse sweating or if he anticipates an evening of energetic dancing.

When wearing a white dress shirt, a gentleman refrains from wearing a T-shirt advertising anything—be it a worthwhile charity, a recent pub crawl, or a center for automotive repair.

A gentleman selects his undershorts, brief or boxer style, according to his own preference, regardless of the event he is attending.

A gentleman replaces his socks and his underwear when they develop holes or when the elastic begins to sag.

A gentleman knows that socks may be darned. His underwear is another matter entirely.

A gentleman does not use his belt as a cinch rope to hoist a pair of slacks that are too large for him.

When putting on his belt, even when he is in a rush, a gentleman always checks to make sure he has not missed a loop.

A gentleman never wears a belt when he is wearing suspenders.

A gentleman never wears suspenders when he is wearing a belt.

A gentleman buys a belt at least one size larger than his pants size.

In almost every case, a gentleman chooses a belt that matches his shoes.

If a gentleman's shoes are some extraordinary color—such as red or blue—he wears a black belt, unless he can find a belt of precisely the same shade of red or blue.

A gentleman understands that only ladies fret over finding a belt to match their red or blue shoes.

No matter how proud a gentleman may be of his rodeo buckle, he wears it only with his jeans.

A gentleman may tighten his belt as severely as he wishes, but by doing so, he impresses only himself and threatens to cut off his circulation.

When the weather is cold, a gentleman always wears gloves, but not just to keep his hands warm. He knows that cold fingers do not make for a pleasant handshake.

Two gentlemen need not remove their gloves when greeting each other with a handshake on a frozen sidewalk or at a football game.

When a begloved gentleman, in the midst of frigid weather, extends his hand to an ungloved person, he makes a simple apology: "Excuse the glove."

Unless he is an usher at a white-tie wedding, or is a banquet waiter, it is highly unlikely that a gentleman will ever be required to wear white gloves.

If a gentleman owns a variety of overcoats, he also owns a variety of gloves to complement them.

A gentleman owns at least one pair of dark leather gloves that he reserves for special occasions.

If he can afford to do so, a gentleman owns an everyday overcoat (perhaps a sturdy trenchcoat) and an overcoat for special occasions (perhaps of camel hair, dark lambswool, or most luxurious, cashmere).

If a married gentleman chooses to wear a ring, he adds only one extra—either a class ring, a simple cameo, or a discreet signet ring.

If an unmarried gentleman elects to wear a ring, he wears only one, selected from the categories mentioned above.

If a gentleman can afford to do so, and if his taste leads him to do so, he may wish to purchase a variety of watches for various occasions and to match different outfits—some in a gold or brass finish, some in silver, some with brown leather bands, some with bands of black leather.

If a gentleman owns only one watch, he owns one he can wear with a suit—and that means one with a classic leather or metal band.

If a gentleman wishes to make scrupulously sure that his watchband matches his belt and other fittings, he purchases a variety of inexpensive silk ribbon bands, in a variety of colors, to make him comfortable on all occasions.

When dressing for business, casual affairs, or formal evenings, a gentleman folds or arranges his pocket square neatly, but with a minimal sense of theater.

The pattern of a gentleman's pocket square never precisely matches the pattern of his necktie.

A gentleman makes sure that he always has a crisply ironed linen pocket square, or two, at his disposal.

A gentleman may wish to equip himself at all times with two handkerchiefs: "one for show, one for blow." The "for show" handkerchief he offers to a lady in distress or to a handkerchiefless friend attacked by a sneezing fit.

If a gentleman proffers his handkerchief to a person attacked by a sudden fit of sneezing or coughing, or if it is needed for reasons of first aid, he does not ask to have the handkerchief returned. If the grateful handkerchief recipient insists on returning the handkerchief, either on the spot or after having it laundered, a gentleman simply says, "No. Thank you. That will be quite all right."

FIVE WAYS TO FOLD A POCKET SQUARE

Pocket Square—One-Point

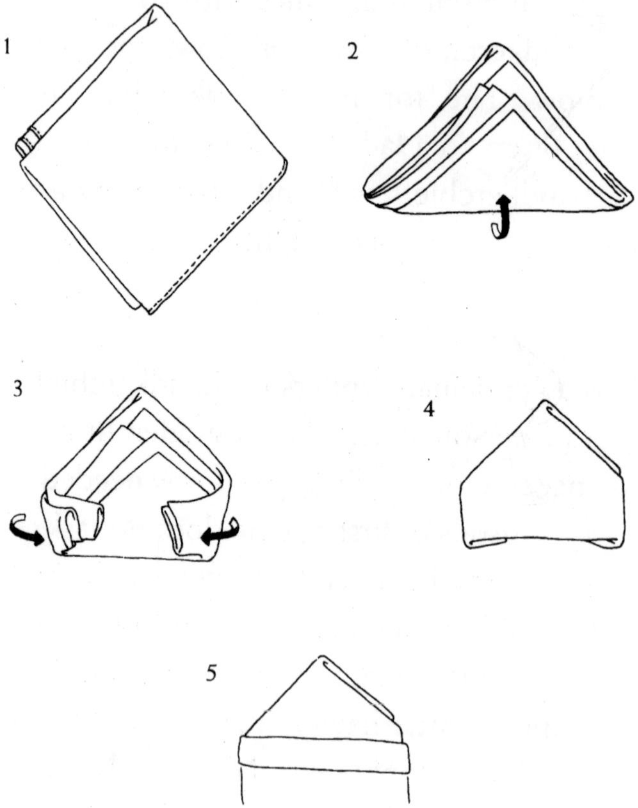

Pocket Square—Two-Point

1

2

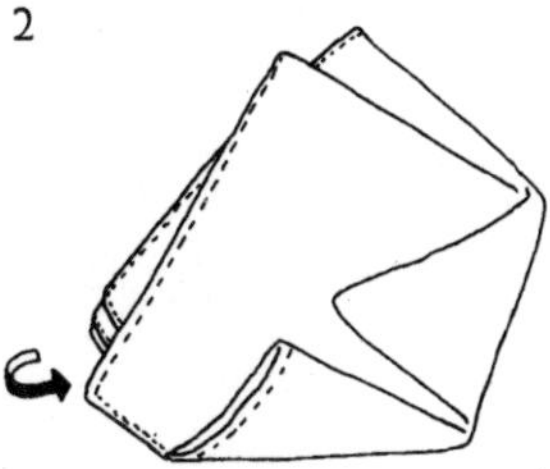

3

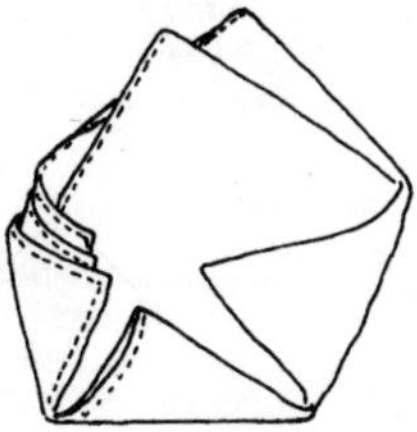

4

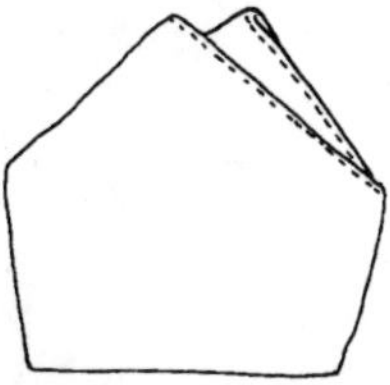

5

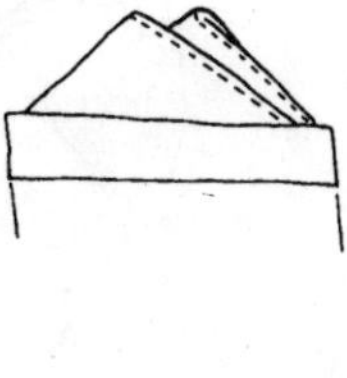

Pocket Square—Flourish

1

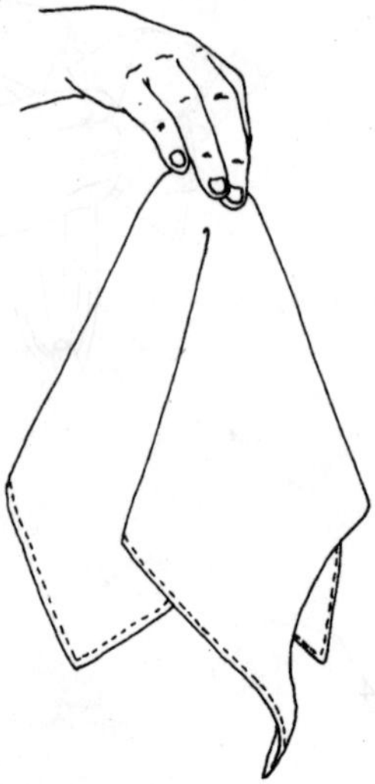

2

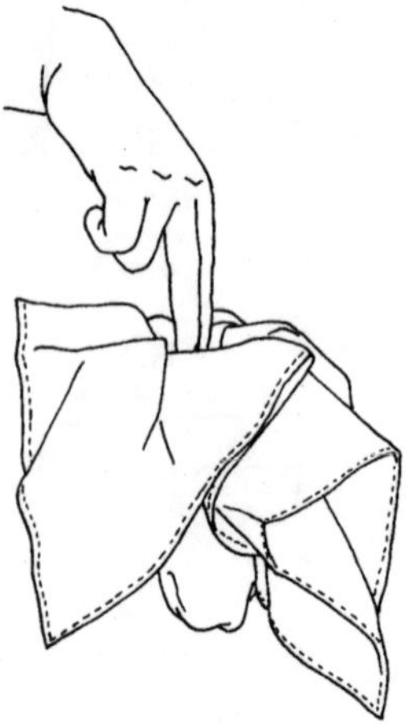

3

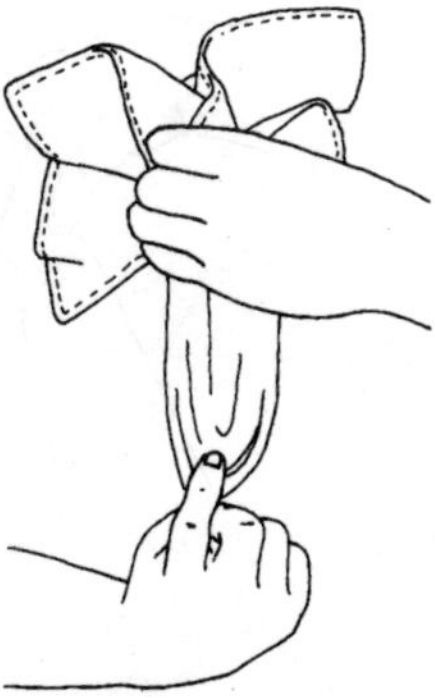

4

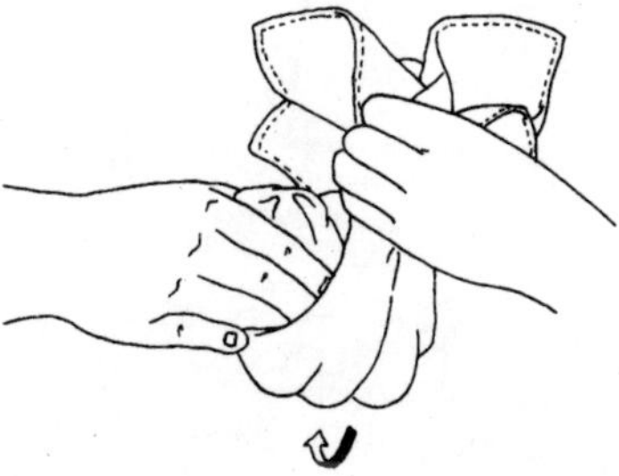

5

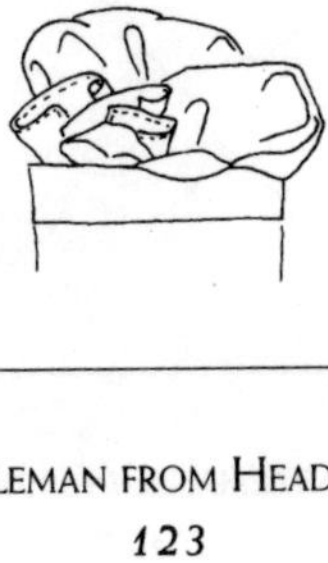

Pocket Square—Multipoint

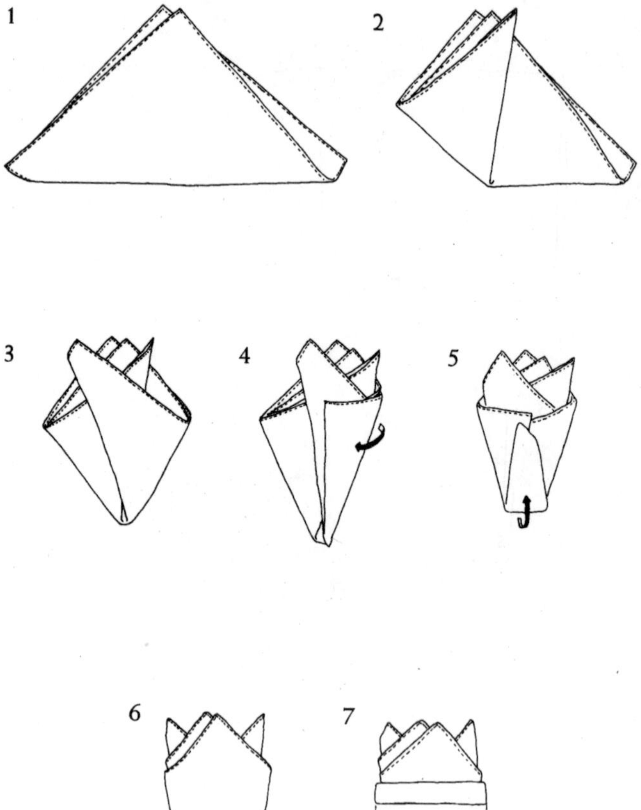

Pocket Square—Banker's Square

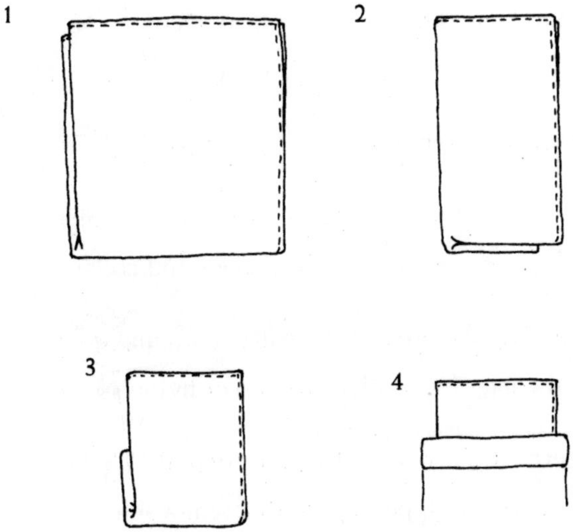

A Gentleman's Glossary: The Finishing Touches

argyle: A diamond-shaped pattern often seen in men's casual socks.

balmacaan: The classic gentleman's overcoat, loosely cut, with a raglan sleeve.

braces: Suspenders, plain and simple.

chesterfield: A gentleman's overcoat in camel hair or wool, with velvet lapels and collar.

clocking: An ornamental pattern running down the leg of a gentleman's silk or nylon socks.

overcoat: A coat, at least knee-length, of heavy wool, perhaps with a removable lining of wool, fur, or some other heavy fabric.

pocket square: A handkerchief, either white linen or colorful silk, intended to be worn only in a gentleman's breast pocket. A pocket square is sometimes smaller than a gentleman's standard pocket handkerchief.

topcoat: A coat roughly the same size as a standard overcoat, but unlined and of a light-wool fabric. A high-quality raincoat and a topcoat are virtually interchangeable.

trenchcoat: A knee-length coat of heavy cotton fabric, replete with belts and epaulets, styled after coats worn in the trenches by officers in World War I.

A Gentleman for All Occasions

A Guide to the Dress Codes of Life

A gentleman understands that the meanings of dress codes differ across the country. He knows that black tie and even white tie are much more common in the South than in other parts of the United States. He knows that in some major cities in the North, for example, such dress is much less frequently seen than in the past—particularly on weeknights. He knows that other than for exceptionally gala evenings, black tie and white tie (or any sort of tie, for that matter) are seldom seen on the West Coast.

If he has received an invitation that does not request he dress formally or in "business attire," a gentleman may feel free to wear his jeans, if he feels most comfortable and handsome in them. Still, he may wish to add a sports coat—and, perhaps, even a tie.

THE DRESS CODES AT A GLANCE

If the Invitation Says . . .	A Gentleman Wears . . .
Black Tie	dinner clothes (tuxedo)
White Tie	evening clothes ("white tie and tails")
Black Tie Optional	a tuxedo or dark suit
Semiformal	a dark suit
Festive Informal	a suit and brightly colored tie
Cocktail Attire	a dark suit or dressy sports coat
Business Attire	a suit and tie
Business Casual	a sports coat; tie is optional
Casual Chic	a sports coat or sweater and slacks
Casual	jeans, slacks, or shorts

A Gentleman Gets Dressed for a Wedding

On those occasions when he must dress himself in preparation to attend a wedding, a gentleman realizes how truly grateful he is that he is not a woman. Given even the most poorly defined dress code, his options are limited. His goal is simply to add to the happiness of the occasion, not to compete for attention among the other guests.

Nevertheless, a wedding is an exceedingly important event in the lives of its central players, so a little decorum may be in order, no matter how casual or rustic the surroundings. If a gentleman is not a member of the wedding party, he may do well to note the following guidelines:

1. If the wedding is scheduled in the late morning or early to mid-afternoon, a gentleman is always appropriately dressed in a dark business suit or in a dark sports coat, dark slacks, and tie—the same outfit he

would adopt, coincidentally, for a funeral. In warm weather, he may choose to wear lighter colored linen, cotton, or seersucker; but only in the South or in resort areas are these options truly risk-free.

2. If a gentleman is invited to a wedding that is to begin later than six o'clock in the evening, he may face the challenge of deciding whether black tie is required. (In such situations, as he will discover, his female companion is highly unlikely to be of help in resolving his dilemma.) At such moments, he may base his decision upon a number of guidelines:
   - He may take a look at the wedding invitation. If the invitation is highly formal in style, decreeing that "Mr. and Mrs. Peyton Scrimshaw Gladsworthy III request the honour of your presence," a gentleman may assume that black tie is appropriate or even expected. (If the wording on the invitation is engraved, on heavy, stiff card stock, a gentleman has even greater reason to assume that dressing up is expected.)
   - A gentleman is well advised to wear his

dinner clothes if he is also invited to the reception following an evening wedding, especially if the site of the reception is an upscale country club or other swell establishment. Nowhere on his invitation or even on the enclosed "reception card" will he see a black-tie dress code prescribed. He simply pulls together the available clues and makes his own assumptions. Even at the most formal wedding and reception, however, he may wear a dark business suit or a dark jacket and slacks.

- Even in the Deep South and even for weddings beginning as late as eight o'clock in the evening, white tie is no longer expected for anyone other than members of the wedding party. And that means *anyone*.
- If a gentleman determines that black tie is the expected dress for the evening, he wears the standard getup—dinner jacket and black trousers with the traditional satin stripe, white formal shirt with good-quality studs and cufflinks, black bow tie, black cummerbund or waistcoat, white

pocket handkerchief, and brilliantly polished (or better yet, patent leather) dancing shoes.

3. For more informal weddings—the sort for which the invitations ask a gentleman to "join Tom and Misty as they toss their communal future to the stars"—a gentleman may dress as he pleases. If he is well acquainted with the couple, he may feel at ease wearing sandals and a fisherman's sweater. If he knows them only because one of the pair is a coworker, he may feel more comfortable in a sports coat and dress shirt—or, in cooler months, a turtleneck.

4. If a gentleman has any doubts as to what he should wear to a wedding—or any other ceremonial occasion, no matter how formal or informal—he feels free to contact his host or hostess, simply asking, "What do you think most of the fellows there will be wearing?" He does not content himself with asking uninformed friends, "Well, Jack, what do *you* think I ought to do?"

DRESSING FOR WEDDINGS . . .

The Wedding Begins at . . .	The Invitation Was . . .
11 A.M.	engraved or thermographed
1 P.M.	photocopied
4 P.M.	e-mailed
5 P.M.	handmade by the bride
5:30 P.M.	printed
7 P.M.	obviously engraved

ANYWHERE, ANY PLACE

THE RECEPTION WILL BE HELD IN . . .	A GENTLEMAN WEARS . . .
a university or alumni club	suit and tie
the VFW hall	sports coat and tie
the groom's favorite sports bar	sports coat and tie
a cow pasture	sandals
the church social hall	sports coat or suit
a major country club or hotel ballroom	black tie

A Gentleman Gets Dressed for a Cocktail Party

As a gentleman goes through life, he learns the distinction between a "cocktail party" and a "cocktail reception." "Reception" implies a rather grand, large-scale occasion, usually staged to welcome the arrival of a new executive at a business institution, a newly appointed official at an academic institution, the ordination or installation of a new clergy person, or the opening of a company's new offices. A reception may also be staged upon the retirement of an executive, official, or clergy person. (Receptions seldom accompany the *closing* of a company's office, no matter what the reason for the closing.)

If an invitation includes the word "reception," it implies a minimal level of formality, requiring that the gentleman wear one of his best business suits or, at the very least, a dark sports coat and somber slacks.

A "cocktail party," on the other hand, is a considerably more casual affair. If a gentleman is invited for cocktails at the home of good friends, he may dress casually, wearing a sweater and none-too-ratty jeans in cold weather or a polo shirt and shorts in the heat of summer. If he receives a written or printed invitation for cocktails, however, he is wise to veer toward the dressy side of casual, adding a sports coat, or even a tie, to his casual slacks or jeans. If he wears a suit on such occasions, a gentleman may feel a tad overdressed, but he is not wrong.

A Gentleman Gets Dressed for a Funeral

When dressing for a funeral, whether he is a member of the mourning family or the attending congregation, a gentleman dresses in the most somber attire he has at hand. Ideally, he wears a dark suit (either black, navy, or dark gray—striped or unstriped); a simple, clean, freshly laundered shirt (white is the most dignified choice); a quiet tie (in a solid color or a simple pattern, eschewing any business logos or clever sayings); dark socks; and black, freshly polished shoes.

At a funeral, in any religious tradition, a gentleman realizes that his personal appearance is of little moment, especially to the bereaved. He dresses quietly, in acknowledgment of that fact.

A Gentleman Gets Dressed for a Religious Service

A gentleman need no longer worry about setting out his suit, tie, shirt, shoes, and socks in preparation for services at his house of worship. Still, it is never wrong for a gentleman to dress as soberly, and somberly, as he wishes when attending any religious service. If he is taking a public role in the service—as an usher, a reader, or leader of the congregational music—he may opt for business suit, tie, and black shoes.

On the other hand, each religious community, whatever its faith or affiliation, has its own, undecreed "dress code." A gentleman may choose either to acknowledge or to disregard that simple reality. At the same time, a gentleman remembers that a religious service, in any faith, is a communal experience. At no time would a gentleman dress in a way that would make him the center of attention—or a reason for comment.

A Gentleman Gets Dressed for a Job Interview

When selecting his clothes for a job interview, a gentleman dresses as he assumes he would dress on a particularly important day at the office, should he be hired for the job he is seeking. If he is interviewing for a job in sales, he wears the sort of outfit he would wear to impress his most prestigious client. If he is interviewing for a job with a law firm, he wears the sort of well-tailored suit and tie he would wear when presenting a crucial argument in court. On the other hand, if he is applying for a job teaching science at the local middle school, he may make a better impression by wearing a good sports coat and nicely cut slacks. In no case does he wish to create an appearance that he cannot keep up or one that suggests he has an overly optimistic impression of the salary being offered. A necktie is appropriate at any job interview.

A Gentleman Gets Dressed for a Concert

Attending an orchestra concert or an opera performance is no longer the semiformal ritual that it once was. Gentlemen in sports coats, pull-over sweaters, and polo shirts are often seen, even in the priciest sections of the house. But since such performances are meant to be a break from the doldrums of workaday life, a gentleman may wish to opt for a dark suit and tie. Unless he is attending a formal event, either before or after the performance—and unless he wishes it to be assumed that he is a member of the cello section—a gentleman feels no obligation to wear black tie to a standard performance by a symphony orchestra or an opera company.

A Gentleman Gets Dressed for a Cookout

For the most casual of parties, a gentleman may dress comfortably in shorts and a polo shirt, a sports shirt, or even a T-shirt. But he makes sure his shorts and his shirt are scrupulously clean and, as much as possible, unwrinkled.

For the most part, when wearing shorts, a gentleman avoids wearing socks, no matter what shoes he has chosen. If he has a great sense of style and particularly slender calves, he may choose to wear socks with his loafers or sandals. He knows, however, that such choices create a strain on his own self-confidence, not to mention the self-confidence of the person he has asked to accompany him for the evening.

A Gentleman Gets Dressed for a Night on the Town

On some evenings, a gentleman does not know where the night will lead him. On such evenings, he thinks ahead, considering the friends with whom he will be traveling and the spots they are likely to frequent.

Unless he has heard that his group may drop in at a dignified social event, a gentleman is wise to stick with a quiet, classic getup (a polo shirt or white oxford-cloth button-down, with jeans or simple slacks and a blazer or dark sports coat).

If the evening's agenda includes a party with a specific dress code (be it black tie or disco), a gentleman sticks to that dress code, explaining, as the evening progresses, why he is dressed inappropriately at that particular moment.

If a gentleman is not willing to make such explanations, he stays home.

A Gentleman Gets Dressed for a White-Tie Fundraiser

The necessity for dressing in "evening clothes," better known as "white tie" is almost dead, except on the most splendid occasions.

Dressing in white tie is an elegant ritual. It has been so ever since its institution, mid-nineteenth century, by that arbiter of gentlemanly style, Beau Brummel. Before Brummel's time, particularly during the flamboyance of the Regency, gentlemen of high society in Britain dressed in the brightest colors they could find, in hopes of attracting attention in crowded ballrooms and at formal salons.

Brummel changed all that, once he had secured his place in Victorian society, simply by arriving at royalty-related and other socially "important" events in his clean, elegantly tailored black swallow-tailed coat and well-fitted black trousers. Once he disdained the prevailing style of flamboyant cravats, scarves, and ties as evening wear for Victorian gentlemen, the last bit of color went out of gentlemanly evening wear forever. And his rule continues—at least when it comes to white-tie evenings.

A gentleman may properly be asked to don white tie as a member of a wedding party for a ceremony that begins at seven o'clock in the evening or later. But he may also find himself invited, on occasion, to charity fundraisers with a white-tie dress code.

If a gentleman chooses to accept this sort of invitation, he also agrees to dress in accordance with the dress code established by Brummel.

He may either purchase or rent

- A black worsted-wool tailcoat, with black buttons
- Black trousers, with a black satin stripe running up the outside of the pants leg
- A white formal shirt with stiffly starched front
- A white waistcoat, with white pearl buttons
- A white bow tie to match the waistcoat
- Black silk or nylon socks
- Black patent leather shoes

A Gentleman Gets Dressed for a Masked Ball

An invitation to a masked ball may note "black tie" as its dress code. Almost invariably, these days, such events are charity benefits. In such cases, a gentleman respects the dress code of the evening, adding almost as an afterthought a simple black half-mask or something a bit more elaborate to fit the theme of the party. On such evenings, a mask is not actually intended as a disguise. Nevertheless, it is intended to add to the color of the night and to suggest that some sort of magic is afoot.

A Gentleman Gets Ready for a Party

When getting dressed for a social occasion of any sort, a gentleman allows himself enough time to do the job right. If he knows that he may be on a tight schedule, he lays his clothes out ahead of time. At the very least, he checks his closet to make sure he has ready access to the clothes he plans to wear. (Otherwise, he may discover that his dinner jacket is still hanging on a rack at the dry cleaner, or his favorite pair of shorts is at the bottom of the laundry hamper.)

In anticipation of a formal occasion, he checks his shoes to make sure they are shined and do not require new soles or heels. He also locates a pair of socks of a matching color or a coordinating pattern.

Because very few gentlemen these days enjoy the services of a valet, on the verge of a formal occasion, a foresightful gentleman inserts his studs into his shirtfront and his cufflinks into his shirt cuffs before he steps into the shower.

Well ahead of time, he buttons his suspenders to his trousers, so that the actual ritual of getting dressed can be as unflurried as possible, allowing him the leisure, perhaps, to sip a light Scotch-and-water as he ties his bow tie.

So that he feels absolutely at ease, in his own body and in the company of others, a gentleman makes sure to use fresh deodorant and brush his teeth (and floss if necessary). He may also wish to rinse with an understated mouthwash, use eye drops (especially if he expects to be in smoky surroundings), and polish his glasses with a good lens cleaner. Except for the deodorant and the tooth brushing, none of these efforts is a necessity. Nevertheless, any of them increases a gentleman's self-confidence, allowing him to walk out the door, fully armed, fully assured, and thoroughly prepared.

A Gentleman Takes Care of His Clothes

A Guide to Preserving Your Investment

A gentleman considers his clothes an investment. He buys the best-quality garments he can afford and has them tailored so that he looks and feels comfortable.

Thus, he does his best to make his clothes last—and look good—for as long as possible. Upon arriving home, he removes his suit jacket or sports coat and drapes it over the back of a chair. He takes off his trousers and lays them across a chair arm. He *never* returns his clothes directly to the closet. Instead, he lets them air out overnight, checking them in the morning for any stains or splotches. When it comes time for him to hang his slacks or his suit pants in the closet, he clips them by their cuffs to a hanger equipped with the necessary grippers. Unless he is trapped in a hotel room where no other option is available, a gentleman never hangs his trousers over a standard hanger. He knows that if he does so, when he needs those trousers again they will require a trip to the ironing board to remove the knee-level creases.

In many cases, and especially if a gentleman's clothes are constructed of high-quality, natural-fiber goods, he may remove stains and splotches by using a clean, lightly dampened washcloth and some delicate rubbing, removing any leftover moistness with a hand-held hair-dryer, turned to the lowest heat setting available.

He knows that it is morsels and dribblings of leftover food that attract moths to his fine wool jackets and slacks. They come to his closet to lay their eggs within the fibers of his jackets, especially in spots already enriched with foodstuff for the moths' emerging larvae. Cedar chips help keep the pests away. Clean jackets do an even better job.

The goal is for a gentleman to send his clothes to the dry cleaner as seldom as possible. Even the highest-quality dry-cleaning operation uses chemicals that attack and weaken fibers—especially synthetics. The seams of some high style suits may even be "fused" rather than stitched, which means, basically, that they have been glued together. Dry-cleaning chemicals are particularly hard on fused seams.

To make matters worse, even high-quality garments are often stitched with synthetic thread that eventually dissolves after being repeatedly subjected to the dry-cleaning process. If a gentleman sends his suits to the dry cleaner after every wearing and begins to note signs of deterioration, the problem is not with the dry cleaner. The problem is his, a problem of poor stewardship and lax maintenance.

Because he may need the skill at any time, a gentleman knows how to sew on a button.

At home, at the office, or when traveling, a gentleman is never without a needle, black and white thread, and a few extra buttons, in a variety of sizes. Even on workday mornings—especially in the few frantic seconds before an important meeting—he will be grateful to have his button-sewing skill and the necessary resources ready at hand.

A gentleman establishes a professional relationship with his dry cleaner, making sure the dry cleaner knows how he prefers his shirts to be starched and how he wishes his pants to be creased.

A gentleman points out any stains or spots on his clothes when he brings them to the dry cleaner. He does not assume his dry cleaner will simply catch them and make them disappear.

A wise gentleman examines his clothes after he picks them up at the laundry or dry cleaner, checking for cracked or lost buttons, ripped pockets, or malfunctioning zippers.

A gentleman does not assume that his dry cleaner is a miracle worker.

A gentleman knows that over time, professional dry cleaning and laundering will take a toll on his clothing.

A gentleman knows his
dry cleaner's name.

A gentleman never hangs his suit or
sports coat on a wire hanger.

A gentleman never hangs his
sweaters on hangers of any sort.

A gentleman uses shoe-trees
even if they are of the most
inexpensive, plastic variety.

A gentleman maintains a
selection of spare shoelaces.

Even if he has thrown away an
old dress shirt, a gentleman
saves the collar stays.

A Gentleman Goes Shopping

A guide to investing in your appearance

A gentleman may like his old clothes. He may, in truth, love them. To him they may feel like comfortable old friends he wishes never to replace. But the time comes when a gentleman has to go shopping. His favorite shirt may have grown frayed around the edges. His one good suit may somehow have shrunk at the waistband. He may actually decide that he would like to come up with a few new choices when he reaches into his closet. Or he may decide that an upcoming social event justifies the challenges of trying on and being fitted. At such moments, a gentleman pays attention to his gut instincts, but he is not afraid to ask for help.

If a gentleman is an inexperienced, or recalcitrant, shopper, he does not attempt to shop in a hurry.

If a gentleman goes shopping for a suit, he makes sure to come back with a suit. He does not become sidetracked by the sale rack of Hawaiian shirts in the corner.

At all times, no matter what the fashion magazines—or the sales clerks—say, a gentleman trusts his own instincts.

A gentleman chooses his sales clerk as carefully as he chooses his attorney, his real estate agent, or his bartender. All three, he knows, are valued confidantes, expected to stand with him through the agonies, excesses, and ecstasies of life.

A gentleman trusts his knowledgeable sales clerk. Yet he is never afraid to ask the dreaded question, "But doesn't it make me look fat?"

If a gentleman thinks it makes him look fat, no matter what anybody else says, he doesn't buy it.

If a gentleman does not like the color, he doesn't buy it.

If a gentleman does not like the pattern, he doesn't buy it.

If a gentleman does not like the price tag, he leaves it alone.

If a gentleman is confident in his own style, he feels comfortable buying new clothes that look and feel much like the old clothes he has at home.

When shopping for clothing in preparation for a special occasion, a gentleman gives himself—and the store—plenty of lead time so that he can consider his decisions and so the store can make any necessary alterations and have the time to get them right.

When a gentleman picks up a garment that has been altered, he tries it on before leaving the store.

A gentleman never returns an item that he has worn, unless he discovers a defect in the item itself or in its alteration.

A gentleman does not return an item simply because he decides, after the fact, that he does not like the style or color. He never does this. Never.

A gentleman shops for his clothes as an investment, in the same way that he shops for his car. He buys the highest quality his budget will allow, confident that it will give him the greatest mileage.

If a gentleman feels he must wait until sale time before buying his suit, he watches for sales at the best-quality stores, where even the sale racks offer suits he will be proud to wear.

If a gentleman buys his suit, jacket, or trousers on sale at a fine establishment, he may be asked to pay for any alterations or tailoring. He does so gladly, knowing that he is still getting a bargain and that the work will be done right.

A gentleman knows that a fine establishment is always concerned about its reputation, no matter whether the merchandise was purchased at full price or on sale.

A gentleman is not intimidated by introducing himself to a fine store at sale time. He and his sales clerk know that there will come a time when he will be able to pay full price.

WAIT A MINUTE! WHO SAYS I WEAR A 54?

UNDERSTANDING THE EUROPEAN SIZE CHART

As more and more clothing is manufactured in Europe—or as more and more clothing manufacturers seem to wish to give that impression—a gentleman may be asked to try on garments labeled with unfamiliar sizes, most of them much larger than anything he has ever before tried on. A gentleman need not be alarmed. A single chart will help him understand the correlatives:

HATS

USA	Europe
6	54
7	56
7¼	58
7½	60
7¾	62

SHIRTS

USA/UK	Europe
14	36
14½	37
15	38
15½	39
16	41
16½	42
17	43
17½	44
18	45

SHOES

USA	UK	Europe
7	6½	40
7½	7	40½
8	7½	41
8½	8	42
9	8½	42½
9½	9	43
10	9½	44
10½	10	44½
11	10½	45
11½	11	46
12	11½	46½

Suits

USA/UK	Europe
36	46
38	48
40	50
42	52
44	54
46	56
48	58

Underwear

USA	Europe
34	5
36	6
38	7
40	8
42	9
44	10
46	11
48	12

RED MEANS STOP, GREEN MEANS GO, OR DOES IT?

A Color-Blind Gentleman Goes Shopping

Approximately one in every twelve men has some form of color blindness. (For every one color-blind woman, there are twenty-five color-blind men.) Sometimes, the affliction is merely bothersome, making it difficult for a gentleman to distinguish deep blues from purples. In the most extreme cases, a gentleman may, in truth, see the world in black and white.

Once a gentleman has acknowledged his color blindness, he may shop just as confidently as any other gentleman, provided he keeps in mind a few helpful hints:

1. A color-blind gentleman is especially careful to develop a trusting relationship with his

sales clerk. He is honest with that person and listens closely to his or her advice.

2. A color-blind gentleman does not go shopping empty-handed. Unless he is absolutely certain that his new suit is black or a classic navy, he takes a swatch of fabric with him. If he can say only, "I think it's sort of gray," he is not helping anyone.

3. When a gentleman buys a new tie or shirt, he simply asks, "Are there other colors with which this would go well?" Before he leaves the store, certainly before he leaves the parking lot, he writes that information down.

4. If a color-blind gentleman receives compliments on a particular outfit, he accepts them graciously. He also makes a mental note. The next time he goes shopping, he tells his favorite sales clerk, "I got a lot of compliments on that new jacket and tie.

What else would you recommend in that direction?"

5. If a color-blind gentleman introduces himself to a sales clerk who says, "Yeah, I'm color-blind too," the gentleman beats a hasty, if tasteful, retreat. He may wish to come back another day. Or he may wish to find another store.

A Gentleman Is Only Human

A guide to surviving life's little fashion emergencies

Even for the best-dressed gentleman, life is likely to have its embarrassing moments. Because he means well, a gentleman knows that none of those moments is actually his fault. Such moments should not invoke inordinate grief, self-loathing, or extended hours with his therapist. A gentleman simply learns from experience and files the moment away for future reference. After all, no matter how expensive the suit, its fly may still be found open at unseemly moments.

A gentleman knows how to zip up and move on.

A GENTLEMAN FACES ADVERSITY

EVEN AT SWELL OCCASIONS, REALLY BAD THINGS HAPPEN

A gentleman may have shopped carefully and confidently, he may have folded his pocket handkerchief crisply, his shoes may be brilliantly shined, and yet . . .

1. **If a gentleman discovers that his fly is open**, he zips it up, right then and there.

2. **If a gentleman notices that another man's fly is open**, he tells him so, right then, on the spot.

3. **If a gentleman spills something on his shirt, jacket, or trousers at a party**, he finds the nearest bartender and asks for a napkin and some soda water. Then he locates the closest

restroom and does his best to repair the damage.

4. **If a gentleman traveler, dressing for a night on the town, discovers that his shirt is missing a button, unless he is equipped (as he should be) with his own needle and thread,** he calls room service. When the replacement button has been provided, and sewn on, he tips extravagantly.

5. **If a gentleman shows up for a social occasion and discovers that he is underdressed,** he acts as if nothing happened amiss. If some thoughtless person should mention that he is a bit too casually dressed, the gentleman makes light of the fact, saying, "Well, my next party is a hayride."

6. **If a gentleman shows up for a social occasion and discovers that he is overdressed,** he makes no mention of the

fact. If the splendor of his attire is mentioned to him and if he is complimented on it (which is likely to be the case), he simply says, "Thanks. I guess I didn't read the dress code."

7. **If a gentleman discovers that he is wearing socks, or even shoes, of two different colors,** he does nothing to draw attention to his mistake. If the occasion is not a seated dinner (during which his mistake would at least be covered by a tablecloth), he makes every attempt to remain standing throughout the evening, lest his blue versus black, or black versus brown misjudgment be all the more evident.

8. **If a gentleman feels that he has been insulted about his appearance,** he ignores the remark, telling himself he misunderstood it. Certainly, he knows, he must have misunderstood the intent of the person uttering it.

9. **If a gentleman discovers that he is sweating profusely, for whatever reason,** he seeks out the nearest source of ventilation and then uses his pocket handkerchief, not his pocket square, to blot his brow. If he is wearing a jacket, he does not remove it (unless he is at a garden party where all the other gentlemen are obviously sharing his suffering). In no case does a gentleman draw attention to the fact that he is dripping with sweat.

10. **If a gentleman discovers that the crotch of his pants, the sleeve of his jacket, or the side of his polo shirt has ripped,** he does not mention the fact, unless the rip is so sizable as to be unavoidable. In such a case, he simply consults the nearest bartender, his host, or even his hostess, requesting a needle and thread. Any such person will likely help him out of his dilemma, even if it means that his host must lend him a shirt, a jacket, or a pair of trousers.

WHAT WAS I THINKING?

TEN THINGS A WELL-DRESSED GENTLEMAN NEVER DOES

1. A gentleman never wears a belt *and* suspenders.

2. A gentleman never wears dress socks with shorts.

3. A gentleman never wears more than one ring (in addition to his wedding band), despite the fact that he may have two hands.

4. A gentleman never shops simply because a sale is in progress.

5. A gentleman never wears a tuxedo that is any color other than black.

6. A gentleman never wears sneakers with a suit—not even with a sports coat, unless jeans are somehow involved.

7. A gentleman never wears a clip-on tie.

8. A gentleman never wears saggy socks that display his shiny shins.

9. A gentleman never wears a jacket he cannot button.

10. A gentleman never demeans another gentleman's apparel.